THE AMERICAN DREAM

Advanced Readings in English

G. Hocmard   M. Sommers

K. A. Sheram   H. Wolff

With reading strategies by Lyn McLean

Consultants: Alphonsine Poujade   J. R. C. Yglesias

Longman

This edition is adapted from "Let's go on! classes terminales"
© Armand Colin - Longman Paris 1978, with the authorization of
Armand Colin - Longman, Paris.

First printing 1982
5 4 3

Longman Inc.
19 West 44th Street
New York, New York 10036
U.S.A.

Distributed in the United Kingdom by Longman Group Ltd., Longman House, Burnt Mill, Harlow, Essex CM20 2JE, England, and by associated companies, branches and representatives throughout the world.

Summary: A collection of more than forty selections portraying life in the United States. Includes exercises to develop reading skills.
1. English language—Text-books for foreigners.
2. Readers—United States.   3. United States—Civilization—Addresses, essays, lectures.
[1. English language—Textbooks for foreigners.
2. Readers.   3. United States—Civilization]
I. Hocmard, G., 1943–
PE1128.A476   428.6'4   82-27
ISBN 0-582-79799-3   AACR2

Printed in the U.S.A.

ILLUSTRATION CREDITS

American Airlines for page 102, American Museum of Natural History for page 49, Mark Antman for pages 43, 63, 68, 69, 72, 78, 92, 112, 125, Bethlehem Steel Corporation for page 66, Bob Bishop for page 61, Black Star, Declan Haun for page 3, Art Buchwald for page 56, Michel Cabaud for page 82, CBS Entertainment for page 115, Cahiers du Cinéma for pages 118, 119, 120, 121, Delta Airlines for page 102, Earl Dotter for page 93, Gamma, David Burnett for page 28, J.P. Laffont for pages 33, 69, 108, 109, Etienne Montés for page 68, Howard E. Harrison for page 42, Howard University for page 39, Jack Knightlinger: The White House for page 123 (right), Magnum, Marc Riboud for page 89, Burk Uzzle for pages 20, 21, Josef Muench for page 75, New York Historical Society for page 37, Peabody Museum of Salem, Massachusetts for page 24, Robert C. Scull for page 127, Sygma, Tony Korody for pages 64, 86, J.P. Laffont for pages 46, 47, Laffont/Franken for page 10, Tiziou for page 19, TWA for page 103, United Airlines for page 103, Washington Post for page 30, Mireille Vautier for page 123 (left).

While every effort has been made to trace the owners of copyright, in a few cases this has proved impossible and we take the opportunity to offer our apologies to any authors whose rights may have been unwittingly infringed. We have been unable to trace the copyright holders of material appearing on pages 11, 20, 35, 53, 57, 79, 93, 105, 123 and 127 and would be grateful for any information that could help us trace them.

Contents

Merritt Parkway - Leverfor   *20*

IV. THE AMERICAN MOSAIC

V. THE AMERICAN WAY OF LIFE

VI. SOCIAL SCENES

PREFACE

The American Dream is probably as intangible as any other dream. Is it an affirmation of traditional American hopes? A cliché, vague and empty of content? Attainable? Forever at the end of the rainbow? This text contains many interpretations of the American Dream. The reading passages reflect the cultural and geographic diversity of the United States as well as the differing viewpoints of American and foreign observers. Some accounts are serious, others whimsical. Some criticize, others eulogize. Included are essays, magazine and newspaper articles, excerpts from novels and plays, poems and interviews—all of which were written at different times in American history and reflect the important issues of the times.

The exercises accompanying each reading are designed to aid in the comprehension of that passage as well as to help students develop reading strategies that can be applied to any text. Exercises are designed to focus on *global meanings, important details* and *key vocabulary items*. Because each passage presents different challenges to the reader, a variety of exercise types has been provided. An overview of the major exercise types follows.

Pre-reading exercises guide students in using their own knowledge or experience to help them **predict** what will follow in an article.

Understanding the Main Idea, Understanding Details and **Locating Specific Information** develop students' abilities to *scan* and *skim* material so that they read more efficiently.

Understanding Vocabulary in Context helps students infer the meaning of unknown words or phrases by using relevant contextual information. This information can come from the meanings of other words in the text or from the students' knowledge of the topic.

Understanding Contextual Reference focuses on important contextual clues such as pronoun reference, noun substitution and ellipsis.

Inferring Meaning guides students in making judgments about the author's purpose and in recognizing different points of view. Other exercises that help students identify inferred meaning are **Recognizing Irony** and **Using Euphemisms.**

Recognizing the Structure of an Argument, Understanding Sequence of Events, Understanding Contrast, Recognizing Examples and Explanations and **Interpreting Language** are exercises on rhetoric that help students understand a passage by focusing on its organization, structure, word choice and style.

Understanding Figurative Language helps students discover how the literal meanings of words in a passage can be extended to metaphorical meanings.

Understanding Syntax assures that students understand the grammatical structures that form the basis for interpreting and understanding the reading.

Composition exercises give students the opportunity to write notes, paragraphs or short essays.

Discussion and **Debate** questions are designed to help students interpret passages and relate their own opinions to what they have read.

1

I. The American Dream...

WHAT DOES IT MEAN ?

An interview with Dr Lee Hertz, 45, a director of a scientific laboratory in Stanford University, California.

INTERVIEWER : What does the expression the American Dream mean to you ?

DR HERTZ : I guess in one way it's the vision of my grandparents. They turned their backs on the poverty and confines of life in Poland in order to integrate themselves and their children into American life.

INTERVIEWER : So the American Dream means getting out of poverty ? 5

DR HERTZ : Then it did. However, when they got to America, they realized that the dream wasn't going to happen, that survival was first. So the dream became the potential for their children to live without hardship.

INTERVIEWER : How could they achieve that ?

DR HERTZ : First through hard work and giving their kids an education. Through 10 education their children would have a choice of being and doing what they wanted. That basically life could be what you made it.

INTERVIEWER : Do you believe that is true ?

DR HERTZ : No, but they did.

INTERVIEWER : Do you mean that you haven't benefitted from the idea of the American 15 Dream ?

DR HERTZ : No, I definitely have. But for me it required rejecting much of the American culture and the kinds of pressure it puts on people. I am talking about financial, material, social and psychological pressures. I haven't wanted to be what my school, my parents and television wanted me to be. 20

INTERVIEWER : But you have had the freedom to pick and choose those elements which have brought you some success, more than your parents ever had.

DR HERTZ : America does give you the opportunity to achieve, though it throws hurdles in your way. However, at least there is room for certain groups of people to be what they want to be and be it successfully. 25

INTERVIEWER : Why do you say a few people ? Isn't the American Dream an idea everyone can believe in ?

DR HERTZ : Yes. But only because our government wants us to believe it. The term American Dream has become a public relations word used to help promote the capitalistic system. It keeps the bulk of the population working and spending their 30 money to acquire things which make the material of the dream.

INTERVIEWER : Well, do they achieve this through hard work ?

DR HERTZ : Of course not. But even if they don't, the constant portrayal of the good life in the mass media, especially T.V., shows that the dream can be reached through money. That's how one learns the American Dream. The constant penetration of 35 advertising which tells you to buy and buy so that finally you will reach the dream.

INTERVIEWER : But if the large part of society doesn't achieve this, why does the idea persist ?

DR HERTZ : Well, since a lot of satisfaction is gained from acquiring things, a considerable amount of people feel they are on the way to achieve what they have 40 been told is available to them through hard work and participation in the American society.

INTERVIEWER : Would you say that it is this goal which makes the system work ?

DR HERTZ : Yes, because people become obsessed with upward mobility, they have to reach the top. They are never satisfied with the status quo. The American Dream is at 45 the end of the rainbow, the end result of the pursuit of happiness. It is the contentment of having sufficient money to buy the things you want, of reaching the status of all the other people who have the money to buy what they want : cars, color T.V.s, washing machines. The American Dream is in one's head and in one's pocketbook. 50

A. UNDERSTANDING CONTEXTUAL REFERENCE. Fill in the blanks.

1. *Then* (line 6) refers to *before Hertz's grandparents came to the U.S.* .
2. *That* (line 9) refers to _____ .
3. *That* (line 13) refers to _____ .
4. *It* (line 30) refers to _____ .
5. *That's* (line 35) refers to _____ .
6. *This goal* (line 43) refers to _____ .

B. UNDERSTANDING FIGURATIVE LANGUAGE. Circle the correct answer.

1. *They turned their backs on the poverty and confines of life in Poland* (lines 2–3) means

   a. they were destroyed by poverty.
   b. they left Poland.
   c. they couldn't leave Poland.

2. People feel *they are on the way to achieve* (line 40) means

   a. they have achieved something.
   b. they can't achieve something.
   c. they are trying to achieve something.

3. *The American Dream is at the end of the rainbow* (lines 45–46) means

   a. the American Dream is something that people can never achieve.
   b. to reach the American Dream people must go through a lot of difficult experiences.
   c. people can achieve the American Dream only when they are very old.

4. *The American Dream is in one's head and in one's pocketbook* (lines 49–50) means

   a. there are two different kinds of American Dreams.
   b. the American Dream is the satisfaction of being able to buy what you want.
   c. the American Dream is different for each person.

C. RECOGNIZING POINTS OF VIEW. Would Hertz agree or disagree with these statements? Write *A* for agree or *D* for disagree.

_____ 1. Anyone who gets a good education can do what he/she wants in life.

_____ 2. Some people can be what they want to be and be successful.

_____ 3. Most people have achieved the American Dream.

_____ 4. The American Dream is a goal that everyone can achieve.

_____ 5. The American Dream is a goal that everyone can believe in.

_____ 6. The meaning of the American Dream has changed a lot in the past 100 years.

_____ 7. The American Dream means more or less the same today as it did 100 years ago.

D. DISCUSSION. Why is money such an important part of the American Dream?

A recording studio in Nashville, Tennessee. Why is the architecture paradoxical?

Paradox and Dream

Americans seem to live and breathe and function by paradox, but in nothing are we so paradoxical as in our passionate belief in our own myths. We truly believe ourselves to be natural-born mechanics and do-it-yourself-ers. We spend our lives in motor cars, yet most of us — a great many of us at least — do not know enough about a car to look in the gas tank when the motor fails. Our lives as we live them would not function without electricity, but it is a rare man or woman who, when the power goes off, knows how to look for a burned-out fuse and replace it. We believe implicitly that we are the heirs of the pioneers; that we have inherited self-sufficiency and the ability to take care of ourselves, particularly in relation to nature. There isn't a man among us in ten thousand who knows how to butcher a cow or a pig and cut it up for eating, let alone a wild animal. By natural endowment, we are great rifle shots and great hunters — but when hunting season opens there is a slaughter of farm animals and humans by men and women who couldn't hit a real target if they could see it. Americans treasure the knowledge that they live close to nature, but fewer and fewer farmers feed more and more people; and as soon as we can afford to we eat out of cans, buy frozen T.V. dinners[1], and jaunt the delicatessens. Affluence means moving to the suburbs, but the American suburbanite sees, if anything, less of the country than the city apartment dweller with his window boxes and his African violets carefully tended under lights. In no country are more seeds and plants and equipment purchased, and less vegetables and flowers raised. [...]

The inventiveness once necessary for survival may also be a part of the national dream. Who among us has not bought for a song an ancient junked car, and with parts from other junked cars put together something that would run? This is not lost; American kids are still doing it. The dreams of a people either create folk literature or find their way into it; and folk literature, again, is always based on something that happened. Our most persistent folk tales — constantly retold in

5

10

15

20

25

books, movies, and television shows — concern cowboys, gun-slinging sheriffs, and Indian fighters. These folk figures existed — perhaps not quite as they are recalled nor in the numbers indicated, but they did exist; and this dream also persists. Even businessmen in Texas wear the high-heeled boots and big hats, though they ride in air-conditioned Cadillacs and have forgotten the reason for the high heels. All our children play cowboy and Indian; the brave and honest sheriff who with courage and a six-gun brings law and order and civic virtue to a Western community is perhaps our most familiar hero, no doubt descended from the brave mailed knight of chivalry who battled and overcame evil with lance and sword. Even the recognition signals are the same; white hat, white armor — black hat, black shield. And in these moral tales, so deepset in us, virtue does not arise out of reason or orderly process of law — it is imposed and maintained by violence. [...]

For Americans too the wide and general dream has a name. It is called "the American Way of Life". No one can define it or point to any one person or group who lives it, but it is very real nevertheless, perhaps more real than that equally remote dream the Russians call Communism. These dreams describe our vague yearnings toward what we wish were and hope we may be : wise, just, compassionate, and noble. The fact that we have this dream at all is perhaps an indication of its possibility.

John Steinbeck : *America and Americans*

---

1. T.V. dinners: prepacked meals on a tray.

A. UNDERSTANDING SYNTAX. Circle the correct answer.

1. *In nothing are we so paradoxical as in our passionate belief in our own myths* (lines 1–2) means

   a. our belief in our own myths is our greatest paradox.
   b. our belief in our own myths is one of our paradoxes, but not the greatest.

2. *Who among us has not bought . . . an ancient junked car* (line 23) means

   a. most of us have bought an old car.
   b. most of us have never bought an old car.

3. *Men and women who couldn't hit a real target if they could see it* (lines 13–14) means

   a. these people can't see very well.
   b. these people can't shoot very well.

4. *These folk figures existed—perhaps not quite as they are recalled nor in the numbers indicated* (lines 29–30) means

   a. these folk heroes existed, but we don't remember them now.
   b. these folk heroes existed, but we don't remember them accurately.

B. UNDERSTANDING CONTRAST. Write the phrase or statement from the text that contradicts each statement below. Note that the conjunctions **but, yet** and **though** indicate contrast.

1. *We spend our lives in motor cars.* (lines 3–4)

   Yet most of us ... do not know enough about a car to look in the gas tank when the motor fails.

2. *Our lives . . . would not function without electricity.* (lines 5–6)

3. *We believe . . . that we have inherited self-sufficiency and the ability to take care of ourselves, particularly in relation to nature.* (lines 7–10)

4. *We are great rifle shots and great hunters.* (line 12)

5. *Americans treasure the knowledge that they live close to nature.* (lines 14–15)

C. DISCUSSION. *No one can define it* [the American Way of Life] *or point to any one person or group who lives it, but it is very real nevertheless, perhaps more real than that equally remote dream the Russians call Communism.* (lines 41–43) Do you agree or disagree? Support your conclusion.

D. COMPOSITION/DISCUSSION. Are people in your country paradoxical as well? What are some of the things people believe in? List as many as you can. Are they all true? Write a composition or discuss your ideas.

Martin Luther King, Sr. at the Lincoln Memorial. Why is it significant that Martin Luther King's father is speaking here?

I Have a Dream

The following are two of the most famous speeches in American history. The first is the address Abraham Lincoln gave at the dedication of a national cemetery at Gettysburg on the site of one of the major battles of the Civil War, four months after thousands had been killed there. The second (slightly shortened) was given a hundred years later by a famous black American, Martin Luther King, Jr., underneath the statue of Lincoln before over a million people who had come to Washington to stage a civil rights demonstration.

The Gettysburg Address

Fourscore and seven years ago our fathers brought forth on this continent, a new nation, conceived in liberty, and dedicated to the proposition that all men are created equal.

Now we are engaged in a great civil war, testing whether that nation, or any

Speech at the Lincoln Memorial

Five score years ago, a great American, in whose symbolic shadow we stand, signed the Emancipation Proclamation. This momentous decree came as a great beacon light of hope to millions of Negro slaves who had been seared in the flames of withering injustice. It came as   5
a joyous daybreak to end the long night of captivity.

But one hundred years later, we must face the tragic fact that the Negro is still not free. One hundred years later, the life of the Negro is still sadly crippled by the manacles of segregation and the chains of discrimination... One   10

nation so conceived and so dedicated, can long endure. We are met on a great battlefield of that war. We have come to dedicate a portion of that field, as a final resting-place for those who here gave their lives that that nation might live. It is altogether fitting and proper that we should do this.

But, in a larger sense, we cannot dedicate — we cannot consecrate — we cannot hallow — this ground. The brave men, living and dead, who struggled here, have consecrated it, far above our poor power to add or detract. The world will little note, nor long remember what we say here, but it can never forget what they did here. It is for us the living, rather, to be dedicated here to the unfinished work which they who fought here have thus far so nobly advanced. It is rather for us to be here dedicated to the great task remaining before us — that from these honored dead we take increased devotion to that cause for which they gave the last full measure of devotion — that we here highly resolve that these dead shall not have died in vain — that this nation, under God, shall have a new birth of freedom — and that government of the people, by the people, for the people, shall not perish from the earth.

Abraham Lincoln
November 19, 1863

hundred years later, the Negro is still languished in the corners of American society and finds himself an exile in his own land. [...]

There will be neither rest nor tranquillity in America until the Negro is granted his citizenship rights. The whirlwinds of revolt will continue to shake the foundations of our nation until the bright day of justice emerges. 15

I say to you today, my friends, that in spite of the difficulties and frustrations of the moment I still have a dream. It is a dream deeply rooted in the American dream. 20

I have a dream that one day this nation will rise up and live out the true meaning of its creed : "We hold these truths to be self-evident; that all men are created equal."

I have a dream that one day on the red hills of Georgia the sons of former slaves and the sons of former 25 slaveowners will be able to sit down together at the table of brotherhood.

I have a dream that one day even the state of Mississippi, a desert state sweltering with the heat of injustice and oppression, will be transformed into an oasis of freedom 30 and justice.

I have a dream that my four little children will one day live in a nation where they will not be judged by the color of their skin but by the content of their character.

I have a dream today. 35

I have a dream that one day the state of Alabama whose governor's [1] lips are presently dripping with the words of interposition and nullification, will be transformed into a situation where little black boys and black girls will be able to join hands with little white boys and white girls and walk 40 together as sisters and brothers.

I have a dream today.

I have a dream that one day every valley shall be exalted, every hill and mountain shall be made low, the rough places will be made plains, and the crooked places will be 45 made straight, and the glory of the Lord shall be revealed, and all flesh shall see it together.[...]

And if America is to be a great nation this must become true. So let freedom ring from the prodigious hilltops of New Hampshire. Let freedom ring from the mighty 50 mountains of New York. Let freedom ring from the heightening Alleghenies of Pennsylvania !

Let freedom ring from the snowcapped Rockies of Colorado !.[...]

Let freedom ring from every hill and mole hill of 55 Mississippi. From every mountainside, let freedom ring.

When we let freedom ring, when we let it ring from every village and every hamlet, from every state and every city, we will be able to speed up that day when all of God's children, black men and white men, Jews and Gentiles, 60 Protestants and Catholics, will be able to join hands and sing in the words of the old Negro spiritual, "Free at last ! free at last ! Thank God Almighty, we are free at last !"

Martin Luther King, Jr., August 28, 1963

1. Governor of Alabama: George Wallace at the time.

A. UNDERSTANDING DETAILS.

Refer to ''The Gettysburg Address'' and circle the correct answer.

1. What happened *fourscore and seven years ago*? (lines 1–2)

   a. The Civil War.
   b. The creation of the United States as an independent nation.
   c. The signing of the Emancipation Proclamation.

2. When was ''The Gettysburg Address'' given? (lines 8–9)

   a. During the Civil War.
   b. After the Civil War.

3. What is *the great task remaining before us*? (lines 39–40)

   a. To honor the dead in this dedication ceremony.
   b. To always remember these dead soldiers.
   c. To work for freedom in the United States.

4. Lincoln's belief that *the world will little note, nor long remember what we say here* (lines 29–31) was

   a. correct.
   b. incorrect.

A young spectator listening to Martin Luther King in August 1963.

B. UNDERSTANDING CONTEXTUAL REFERENCE.

Refer to the ''Speech at the Lincoln Memorial'' and fill in the blanks.

1. *A great American in whose symbolic shadow we stand* (lines 1–2) refers to _____ *Abraham Lincoln* .

2. *This momentous decree* (line 3) refers to _____ .

3. *His own land* (line 13) refers to _____ .

4. *These truths* (lines 22–23) refers to _____ .

5. *A nation* (line 33) refers to _____ .

6. *This* (line 48) refers to _____ .

7. *We* (last line) refers to _____ .

C. UNDERSTANDING STYLES OF SPEECH. These two speeches are in an oratorical style. If Martin Luther King had been giving an interview to a journalist after his speech, he probably would have expressed himself differently. Compare these sentences:

> • *Five score years ago, a great American, in whose symbolic shadow we stand, signed the Emancipation Proclamation.*
>
> • Abraham Lincoln signed the Emancipation Proclamation a hundred years ago.

Write the meaning of these sentences from the "Speech at the Lincoln Memorial."

1. *One hundred years later, the life of the Negro is still sadly crippled by the manacles of segregation and the chains of discrimination . . .* (lines 8–10)

_____

_____

2. *The whirlwinds of revolt will continue to shake the foundations of our nation until the bright day of justice emerges.* (lines 16–18)

_____

_____

3. *. . . one day this nation will rise up and live out the true meaning of its creed.* (lines 21–22)

_____

_____

4. *. . . the sons of former slaves and the sons of former slaveowners will be able to sit down together at the table of brotherhood.* (lines 25–27)

_____

_____

5. *. . . even the state of Mississippi, a desert state sweltering with the heat of injustice and oppression, will be transformed into an oasis of freedom and justice.* (lines 28–31)

_____

_____

6. *. . . the state of Alabama, whose governor's lips are presently dripping with the words of interposition and nullification . . .* (lines 36–38)

_____

_____

7. *. . . little black boys and black girls will be able to join hands with little white boys and white girls and walk together as sisters and brothers.* (lines 39–41)

_____

_____

8. *I have a dream that one day every valley shall be exalted, every hill and mountain shall be made low, the rough places will be made plains, and the crooked places will be made straight, and the glory of the Lord shall be revealed, and all flesh shall see it together.* (lines 43–47)

_____

_____

D. DISCUSSION. In what ways do you think Abraham Lincoln and Martin Luther King express the American Dream?

> *Here in America are all the wealth of soil, of timber, of mines and of the sea put into the possession of a people who wield all those wonderful machines, have the secret of steam, of electricity; and have the power and habit of invention in their brain. — American energy is overriding every venerable maxim of political science. America is such a garden of plenty, such a magazine of power that at her shores all the common rules of political economy utterly fail. Here is bread and wealth and power and education for every man who has the heart to use his opportunity.*
>
> **From *Resources* by R. W. Emerson**

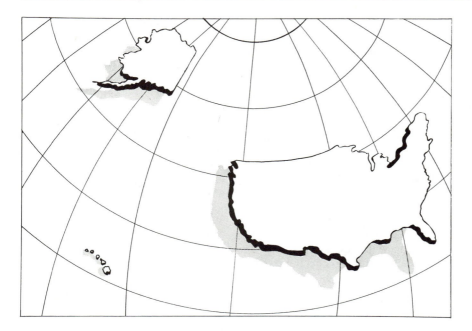

A Slice of a Continent

Over 200 million people whose ancestors came from all of the continents, many races, many climates, lakes, mountains, valleys, fields—how can anyone describe America, or what it means to be an American? John Dos Passos, one of America's great writers, tries. The following is an extract from the introduction to his U.S.A.: The 42nd Parallel.

The young man walks by himself searching through the crowd with greedy eyes, greedy ears taut to hear, by himself, alone.

The streets are empty. People have packed into subways, climbed into streetcars and buses; in the stations they've scampered for suburban trains; they've filtered into lodgings and tenements, gone up in elevators into apartmenthouses. In a showwindow two sallow windowdressers in their shirtsleeves are bringing out a dummy girl in a red evening dress, at a corner welders in masks lean into sheets of blue flame repairing a cartrack, a few drunk bums shamble along, a sad streetwalker fidgets under an arclight. From the river comes the deep rumbling whistle of a steamboat leaving dock. A tug hoots far away.

The young man walks by himself, fast but not fast enough, far but not far enough (faces slide out of sight, talk trails into tattered scraps, footsteps tap fainter in alleys); he must catch the last subway, the streetcar, the bus, [...] register at all the hotels, work in the cities, answer the wantads, learn the trades, take up the jobs, live in all the boarding-houses, sleep in all the beds. One bed is not enough, one job is not enough, one life is not enough. At night, head swimming with wants, he walks by himself alone. [...]

Only the ears busy to catch the speech are not alone; the ears are caught tight, linked tight by the tendrils of phrased words, the turn of a joke, the singsong fade of a story, the gruff fall of a sentence; linking tendrils of speech twine through the city blocks, spread over pavements, grow out along broad parked avenues, speed with the trucks leaving on their long night runs over roaring highways, whisper down sandy byroads past wornout farms, joining up cities and fillingstations, round-houses, steamboats, planes groping along airways; words call out on mountain pastures, drift slow down rivers widening to the sea and the hushed beaches.

It was not in the long walks through jostling crowds at night that he was less alone, or in the training camp at Allentown, or in the day on the docks at Seattle, or in the empty reek of Washington City hot boyhood summer nights, or in the meal on Market Street[1], or in the swim off the red rocks at San Diego, or in the bed full of fleas in New Orleans, or in the cold razorwind off the lake, or in the gray faces trembling in the grind of gears in the street under Michigan Avenue[2], or in the smokers of limited expresstrains, or walking across country, or riding up the dry mountain canyons, or the night without a sleepingbag among frozen beartracks in the Yellowstone, or canoeing Sundays on the Quinnipiac;

but in his mother's words telling about longago, in his father's telling about when I was a boy, in the kidding stories of uncles, in the lies the kids told at school, the hired man's yarns, the tall tales the doughboys told after taps;

it was the speech that clung to the ears, the link that tingled in the blood; U.S.A.

U.S.A. is the slice of a continent. U.S.A. is a group of holding companies, some aggregations of trade unions, a set of laws bound in calf, a radio network, a chain of moving picture theatres, a column of stock-quotations rubbed out and written in by a Western Union[3] boy on a blackboard, a publiclibrary full of old newspapers and dogeared historybooks with protests scrawled on the margins in pencil. U.S.A. is the world's greatest rivervalley fringed with mountains and hills. U.S.A. is a set of bigmouthed officials with too many bankaccounts. U.S.A. is a lot of men buried in their uniforms in Arlington Cemetery[4]. U.S.A. is the letters at the end of an address when you are away from home. But mostly U.S.A. is the speech of the people.

John Dos Passos : *The 42nd Parallel*

---

1. Market Street: in San Francisco. 2. Michigan Avenue: in Chicago. 3. Western Union: telegram company. 4. Arlington Cemetery: National Military Cemetery near Washington, D.C.

A. UNDERSTANDING THE MAIN IDEA. Circle the correct answer.

1. In paragraph 2

   a. it is morning.
   b. it is evening.

2. The main idea of paragraph 3 is

   a. the young man is in a hurry to get home.
   b. Americans want as many experiences in life as possible.

3. Paragraph 4 is

   a. a description of the sounds that can be heard in the city and country.
   b. a description of the different ways that people speak.

4. According to the last four paragraphs of the reading, the main characteristic that identifies the United States as one country is

   a. a similar geography.
   b. a common history.
   c. the way the people speak.

B. COMPOSITION.
The author presents one picture of the USA. What does the USA mean to you? List all the ideas and images you can think of. Then write a composition on your impression of the USA.

C. DISCUSSION.
In what ways could the passage be considered more a poem than a narrative?

LOVING AMERICA

Loving America is a very special task. No other country makes quite the same demands in being loved, nor presents quite the same difficulties.

In most other nations, patriotism is essentially the love of family, of tribe, of land, magnified. There may well be an ideological mixture. The France of the Revolution and Napoleon, for instance, proclaimed the rights of man. Liberty, equality, fraternity were useful enough to overthrow an order and kill a king. But France's love of her earth and her produce, her landscape, her language and her money — those are the things French patriotism is really about. So it is with other European nations. The songs and the poetry of patriotism are filled with scenery: with rivers and mountains, with cities longed for, with valleys lost, with castles conquered. American patriotism has much less of this specific sense of place. [...]

It is possible to be deeply moved by the endless American plains, and the settlements defiantly set down in the midst of this vastness, by the coast of Maine or the Rockies or the desert. But that is not loving America. Loving America means loving what it stands for as a political and social vision. Although the great American epic is the conquest and taming of a continent, American patriotism is not concentrated on geography but on a historic event and an idea. The event is the creation of the United States as a fresh start [...]. The idea is freedom. Both notions have been distorted or perverted at times — that happens with all patriotism. But even when it is misused, American patriotism remains ideological more than racial or ethnic.

When the French carved up Germany or the Germans carved up France, it was done for the greater glory of each nation, with firm belief in the innate superiority of their own people. Whenever Americans went to war, they may have been seized by jingoism to some extent, but more than anything else Americans believed they were fighting for ideas, for a system. It may have been naive to think that other countries were waiting to be given the blessings of democracy, free enterprise and individualism, but that is what Americans did believe.

The U.S. was not born in a tribal conflict, like so many other nations, but in a conflict over principles. Those principles were thought to be universal, which was part of the reason for the unprecedented policy of throwing the new country open to all comers. [...] The millions from other lands and other cultures had different loves for many different plots of earth, languages, traditions. The unifying love had to be for America as an idea.

In part, this helps to explain the unusual stability of American institutions. In Europe it is possible to shift loyalties from king to republic, from democracy to dictatorship, and still love one's country. In the U.S. loyalty must be to the institutions themselves. [...]

We still perceive America as something unprecedented in history, as an experiment, and as such something that must "work" in order to prove itself over and over again. Hence America demands that love be given not once and for all, but that it be constantly renewed and reaffirmed. [...] "My country, right or wrong" is not a very American slogan. We Americans have a hard time accepting a situation in which our country is wrong, not because we are more arrogant than other people, but because our country's rightness is our soil, our home. [...]

One loves America both for its virtues and its faults, which are deeply intertwined. Indeed, one loves America for the virtues of its faults.

One loves the almost obsessive American need to believe, the resistance to cynicism even if that sometimes means oversimplification and moralizing. One loves the unique American restlessness, the refusal to settle for what is, even if that sometimes means a lack of contemplation and peace. One loves the fact that America sees itself as the shaper of its own destiny, both private and public. [...] This rejection of fate, this insistence that everything is possible, is surely the dominant American characteristic, and at the heart of its genius. [...]

In rejecting fate, the U.S. is the ultimate incarnation of Western, Faustian man. [...] Disease, poverty and other ancient afflictions simply are not accepted as part of the human condition. Perhaps rightly so — and yet the conviction that they can be banished completely is a tremendous burden because each setback, each delay, is seen as a personal or national failure. That is partly why we Americans are so impatient with the study of history — because history is a reminder of fate. We would rather learn to do than learn to know.

One must love this American view of learning as the tool by which man transforms himself. We Americans believe that everything can be learned, including, to a very large extent, to be what you are not. [...] There is something admirable about this, yet nagging questions remain. Where is the line between making the most of one's potential and reaching for the unattainable? [...]

The American spirit is deeply divided about money. In one sense the faith in money is pure: it need not, as it does in so many older societies, apologize for its existence. Money is what it is — good in its own right, a sign of success, if perhaps no longer of divine grace. Yet this conflict is at war with an older tradition [...]. The great callings are not trade or commerce but the state or the military or the church or scholarship. The great legendary virtues are not thrift — and its explosive extension, profit — but courage, kindness, faith. [...]

Ultimately all American forces, including money, converge in the passion for freedom. [...]

We tend to think of freedom as a positive and unalloyed good. We speak of "enjoying" freedom. [...] It can be argued that we bear freedom for much of the rest of the world — not only in the sense of material and military support for the cause of freedom as the West understands it, but in the sense of experimenting with freedom in a kind of vast social laboratory. [...]

For freedom to be workable and social system, strong inr a powerful moral compass values, are needed. In p contradiction is vast. The increasingly hard to read, hard to find in a frantically open, mobile, fractioned society. Thus, a troubling, paradoxical question: Does freedom destroy the inner disciplines that alone make freedom possible? [...]

One loves America for its accomplishments as well as for its unfinished business. [...] One ultimately loves America not for what it is, or what it does, but for what it promises. [...]

Henri Grunwald in *Time*,
July 5, 1976

A. UNDERSTANDING DETAILS. Circle the correct answer.

1. *Patriotism* in America (paragraph 2) means

    a. liberty, equality and fraternity.
    b. love of earth, produce, landscape, language and money.
    c. the possibility to begin again and love of freedom.

2. According to the author (paragraph 3), America has gone to war

    a. for the glory of the nation.
    b. to defend democracy, free enterprise and individualism.
    c. to win tribal conflicts.

3. American institutions are more stable than those in Europe (paragraph 5) because

    a. America is full of people who came from so many different countries.
    b. to believe in America means to believe in its institutions.
    c. there are many more institutions in America.

4. *"My country right or wrong"* (paragraph 6) is not a very American slogan because

    a. Americans must believe that the principles on which their country is based are right.
    b. Americans are not arrogant people.
    c. America has very stable institutions.

5. Americans are impatient with the study of history (paragraph 9) because

    a. historical accounts are not always accurate.
    b. they don't want to be reminded of man's limitations.
    c. history uncovers national failures.

6. Americans believe (paragraph 11) that

    a. it is bad to have too much money.
    b. making money is the most important goal in life.
    c. money is one of the signs of success.

B. **RECOGNIZING EXAMPLES AND EXPLANATIONS.** Write the examples or explanations found in the text.

1. Three examples of *the rights of man*. (paragraph 1)
liberty, equality and fraternity

2. An explanation of *jingoism*. (paragraph 3)
_____

3. An explanation (three characteristics) of *the system* the Americans believed they were fighting for. (paragraph 3)
_____

4. Two examples of America's *virtues of its faults*. (paragraphs 7–8)
_____
_____

5. Two examples of *ancient afflictions*. (paragraph 9)
_____

6. Four examples of *the great callings*. (paragraph 11)
_____

7. Three examples of *the great legendary virtues*. (paragraph 11)
_____

C. **DISCUSSION**

1. *One loves America both for its virtues and its faults, which are deeply intertwined.* (paragraph 7) Can the same be said about your country? What do you think some of the virtues and faults of your country are?

2. *Does freedom destroy the inner discipline that alone makes freedom possible?* (next to last paragraph) Discuss Grunwald's point of view and your own.

3. Defend the statement *American patriotism remains ideological more than racial or ethnic*. (paragraph 2) Use arguments from the text.

AMERICA – love it or leave it!

THE DECLARATION OF INDEPENDENCE

The Making of the Declaration of Independence.

When in the Course of Human Events it becomes necessary for one people to dissolve the political bands which have connected them with another, and to assume among the Powers of the earth, the separate and equal station to which the Laws of Nature and of Nature's God entitle them, a decent respect to the opinions of mankind requires that they should declare the causes which impel them to separation.

We hold these truths to be self-evident, that all men are created equal, that they are endowed by their Creator with certain unalienable Rights, that among these are Life, Liberty and the pursuit of Happiness.

That to secure these rights, Governments are instituted among Men, deriving their just powers from the consent of the governed, That whenever any Form of Government becomes destructive of these ends, it is the Right of the People to alter or to abolish it, and to institute a new Government, laying its foundation on such principles, and organizing its powers in such form, as to them shall seem most likely to effect their Safety and Happiness.

A. RECOGNIZING THE STRUCTURE OF AN ARGUMENT. Circle the correct answer.

1. Which of these points does *not* appear in paragraph 1?

   a. The United States is declaring itself independent from Britain.
   b. The United States is forming a separate nation equal to Britain.
   c. The people of the United States are entitled to three basic rights by the Laws of Nature and of Nature's God.
   d. The United States respects the opinions of mankind.

2. Which of these points does *not* appear in paragraph 2?

   The rights that cannot be taken from men are
   a. Life.
   b. Liberty.
   c. Fraternity.
   d. the pursuit of happiness.

3. Which of these points does *not* appear in paragraph 3?

   a. Governments get their power from the people who are governed.
   b. If governments don't secure these basic rights, they may be abolished by the people.
   c. There is a specific procedure by which governments should be abolished.
   d. People may create a new government which is more advantageous to them.

MERRITT PARKWAY

As if it were
forever that they move, that we
keep moving —
Under a wan sky where
as the lights went on a star
pierced the haze and now
follows steadily
a constant
above our six lanes
the dreamlike continuum...

And the people — ourselves!
the humans from inside the
cars, apparent
only at gasoline stops
unsure,
eyeing each other
drink coffee hastily at the
slot machines and hurry
back to the cars
vanish
into them forever, to
keep moving —

II. ... Reaching for It

Houses now and then beyond the
sealed road, the trees/trees, bushes
passing by, passing
      the cars that
            keep moving ahead of
us, past us, pressing behind us
                     and
             over left, those that come
         toward us shining too brightly
moving relentlessly

      in six lanes, gliding
north south, speeding with
a slurred sound —

Denise Levertov: *The Jacob's Ladder*

MOVING TO THE SUNBELT

An interview with Jim Studebaker, 39, born in Ohio and trained in New York to be a photographer. He recently moved to Santa Fe, New Mexico.

INTERVIEWER : What made you decide to leave New York ?

JIM : Well, for one thing, I couldn't stand the rat race.

INTERVIEWER : Do you mean the competition ?

JIM : It was not so much that as the pace of things. In New York with the subway and commuter train schedules, I was constantly looking at my watch.

INTERVIEWER : How are things different now ?

JIM : For one thing, my productivity is sky high. In New York I spent a lot of my life being busy, but not really doing much, you know. Now I am busy and producing good things. Before I left New York I had reached the end of my emotional and professional strength. Now, everything about my life seems to have changed. First of all it's more relaxing and informal here. I feel in touch with people around me. When I got to Santa Fe I found people with casual manners, easy and loose in their movements instead of the pressurized people and skyscrapers bearing down on me.

INTERVIEWER : Does that mean that you no longer feel crowded in ?

JIM : Well, yes, that's part of it. People give you a lot of elbow room. And besides the pacing of things is different. Things don't seem so rushed. It's more relaxing and informal here. There's less pressure on people so they can concentrate more on what they want to really do in life. Santa Fe has given me more freedom than any place I've ever been.

INTERVIEWER : But what about the cultural and intellectual stimulation of a place like New York. Don't you miss that ?

JIM : Not really. I visited New York recently but left after two days. That was all I could stand. I started getting that closed-in feeling again. Here in the Sunbelt there is room to grow. The climate is pleasant.

INTERVIEWER : Do you think your children are better off here ?

JIM : And how ! This is a great place to raise children. They can get a real sense of freedom, being outdoors, establishing healthy relationships with their environment and us too.

INTERVIEWER : So you are happy with your move, you don't miss the movement and attractions of a big city ?

JIM : Not at all. This is really where the action is. People have been saying for years that the Southwest is the new frontier in America, where people can still reach the American Dream. It's certainly been true for me.

A. UNDERSTANDING VOCABULARY IN CONTEXT. Circle the correct answer.

1. *I couldn't stand the rat race* probably means

   a. I didn't like all the competition.
   b. it was impossible to get from place to place because subway and train transportation was so poor.
   c. I felt nervous and under pressure because things happened so quickly.

2. *My productivity is sky high* means

   a. I'm very busy.
   b. I'm getting a lot done.
   c. I'm really excited about what I'm doing.

3. *I feel in touch with people around me* means

   a. it's easy to communicate with people.
   b. there are a lot of people around me.
   c. there is a lot more physical contact with people.

4. *People give you a lot of elbow room* means

   a. people don't try to pressure you.
   b. people stay away from you.
   c. people are always touching you.

5. *The pacing of things is different* means

   a. life is slower.
   b. life is less expensive.
   c. there's more freedom.

6. *I started getting that closed-in feeling again* means

   a. I felt pressured.
   b. I felt restless.
   c. I felt afraid.

B. DISCUSSION. *In New York I spent a lot of my life being busy, but not really doing much.* Do you feel this is true of your life or of the people around you? Why or why not?

Advertisement for a sailing ship from New York to California. How do you think such advertisements helped encourage the Gold Rush?

The Gold Rush

One prime wonder of the California gold rush is that so many people survived it. They poured out of Atlantic seaboard[1] cities, Ohio villages and Southern plantations in abysmal ignorance of the geographic and social obstacles that loomed ahead. Had the deluge dropped onto an unprepared California, the results would have been disastrous. Thanks to the continent's width, however, men who were familiar with the West had a year's grace during which they could attack the knottier problems connected with geology, mining technology, transportation, and political order that were raised by the frenzy.

Even among experienced Westerners, the madness was acute. "The whole country," wrote one San Francisco newspaper editor, "[...] resounds with the sordid cry of gold! GOLD! GOLD! while the field is left half planted, the house half built, and everything neglected but the manufacture of shovels and pick axes." The alcalde of Monterey described the situation there: "All were off for the mines, some on horses, some on carts, and some on crutches, and one went in a litter."

Breathless talk like that suggests, inaccurately, that torrents of people washed immediately through the mountains. Actually, the rush developed slowly. In mid 1848, California's non-Indian population, women and children included, amounted to no more than fourteen thousand. Perhaps half of these were native *Californios*, many of them living on isolated ranches in the south and less susceptible to the fever than the Americans and Englishmen in the towns farther north. Probably there were no more than a thousand people who were directly involved with the initial rush.

New surges soon followed, however, as fast as ships spread the news along the Pacific shores. The first groups appeared during the summer from Hawaii — nineteen vessels in three weeks. Their clamour for supplies sent prices skyrocketing. Flour that sold for twenty dollars a barrel at Stockton early in the summer, soared in the mountains, during moments of pinch, to eight hundred dollars. Eggs at times brought three dollars each. [...]

The thousand Californians who hurried toward the mountains during that first spring of 1848 lived in pure romance. They climbed from hot valleys into rolling hills dotted with live oaks and vivid with orange poppies. The canyons deepened, singing with water. No rain came until late fall; they camped in comfort under the flimsiest shelters of brush, or under nothing at all. The great drawback was a dearth of food. Hunting took time, and as a result, the length of a man's stay in the diggings was determined by what he could carry with him.

Even the climate cooperated. The annual summer drought shrank the streams, exposing deposits of gold-bearing gravel called bars. These had formed during high water wherever the current was slack: opposite bends in the river channel, behind boulders, and in potholes in the stream bed. Gold had settled with the gravel. Heavier than the sand, it worked its way into cracks and cavities in or near bedrock. Receding water opened these spots to the crude tools of the early miners. Other deposits were found in ancient channels that had been left dry following changes in the stream's course.

Rewards were sometimes extraordinary. One lump of gold unearthed at Sonora weighed twenty-eight pounds; eight other nuggets from the same district exceeded twenty pounds. A small group of friends from Monterey, aided by hired Indians, took two hundred and seventy pounds from the Feather River in seven weeks. The first five prospectors to reach the Yuba River gleaned seventy-five thousand dollars in three months. In ten days one soldier off on a furlough picked up fifteen hundred dollars. These strikes and similar ones in '49 and even '50 were exceptions; yet even those unoriginal souls who clung near the familiar bars at Coloma, the site of Marshall's[2] discovery, are said to have averaged twenty-five to thirty dollars a day, at a period when skilled labour elsewhere in California commanded about three dollars daily. Under such conditions, a man did not mind standing in icy water all day while a hot sun beat on his head, his shoes turned to pulp, and his stomach, assaulted with insufficient amounts of monotonous food, sent forth calls of distress.

David Lavender: *The Penguin Book of the American West*

---

1. Atlantic seaboard: the northeastern states. 2. Marshall: the discoverer of the first nugget.

A. **UNDERSTANDING SEQUENCE OF EVENTS.** How did the California gold rush progress? Number the sentences in chronological order.

_____ Nineteen vessels arrived from Hawaii.

_____ A thousand Californians rushed to the mountains.

_____ The cost of flour, eggs and other supplies increased drastically.

_1_ People left their homes in the East, South and Middle West and headed for California to look for gold.

B. **UNDERSTANDING DETAILS.** Write *T* for true or *F* for false as shown in the example. Then underline the information in the passage that your answer is based on.

_F_ 1. People coming to hunt for gold knew a lot about California.

> They poured out of Atlantic seaboard cities, Ohio villages and Southern plantations in abysmal ignorance of the geographic and social obstacles that loomed ahead.

_____ 2. It took over two years for the first groups of people from the East to arrive in California.

_____ 3. Almost all of the people looking for gold were from outside California.

_____ 4. Native *Californios* were Indians.

_____ 5. The ships full of people looking for gold also brought lots of supplies.

_____ 6. In the spring of 1848 there was very little food in the mountains.

_____ 7. Bars containing gold form in parts of the river where there isn't much movement in the water.

_____ 8. The miners had complicated equipment.

_____ 9. Almost every miner found gold and made money.

_____ 10. Looking for gold was pleasant, easy work.

C. UNDERSTANDING VOCABULARY IN CONTEXT. Circle the correct answer.

1. *Knottier* problems (paragraph 1) are

    a. easier problems.
    b. more difficult problems.

2. A *frenzy* (paragraph 1) is

    a. a discovery.
    b. a crazy, confusing situation.

3. *Madness was acute* (paragraph 2) means

    a. everyone was very crazy.
    b. a few people were doing things that were a little crazy.

4. *Moments of pinch* (paragraph 4) are

    a. ways of measuring flour.
    b. difficult times.

5. A *drawback* (paragraph 5) is

    a. an advantage.
    b. a disadvantage.

6. A *dearth of food* (paragraph 5) means

    a. there is a lot of food.
    b. there isn't a lot of food.

7. *Nuggets* (paragraph 7) are

    a. miners.
    b. lumps of gold.

D. DISCUSSION. Who do you think made the most money in the California gold rush? Justify your answer.

CLEMENTINE

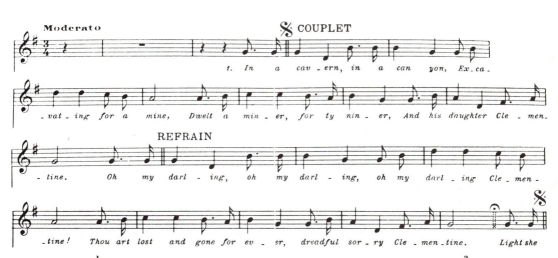

1
In a cavern, in a canyon,
Excavating for a mine,
Dwelt a miner, forty niner,
And his daughter Clementine.
  Oh my darling, etc.

2
Light she was and like afairy,
And her shoes were number nine,
Herring boxes without topses,
Sandals were for Clementine.
  Oh my darling, etc.

REFRAIN
Oh my darling, oh my darling,
Oh my darling Clementine!
Thou art lost and gone for ever,
Dreadful sorry Clementine.

3
Drove she ducklings to the water,
Every morning just at nine,
Hit her foot against a splinter,
Fell into the foaming brine.
  Oh my darling, etc.

4
Saw her lips above the water
Blowing bubbles mighty fine,
But alas! I was no swimmer,
So I lost my Clementine.
  Oh my darling, etc.

Panning for gold today.

BONANZA 77

What the Federal Government could not know when they lifted the ban on private ownership of gold in 1975 was that the resulting increase in the price of the metal from $35 to $145 an ounce would trigger an epidemic of long-forgotten gold fever.

Two years after, virtually every old mining area in the country is the site of a weekend rush, with starry-eyed tourists pouring in with portable dredges in their arms and hope in their hearts. The most crowded, naturally, is the Mother Lode in Northern California where the 1849 Gold Rush began when John Marshall discovered a tiny gold rock at John Sutter's mill near the American Fork. Over the years it has produced an estimated billion dollars' worth of gold, but geologists are convinced that there is even much more to be found.

The only investment required from the amateur prospector is a portable dredge (currently selling for $160) that sucks in the sand and gravel, separates the heavier rocks, some of which might turn out to be golden nuggets. With a minimum skill, virtually no effort, and admittedly some luck, a prospector can make $200 or more on a single weekend. This is not "striking it rich", but it certainly is a nice way to "enrich your leisure time"; and at least for the motel and restaurant owners in the area, it *is* a bonanza.

Ed Pinchbeck in
The Eastern Orleans Gazette and Telegraph, Aug. 4, 1977

One Woman's Empire

A. PREDICTING. Read the first paragraph of this article.
What do you think it will be about? Circle the best answer.

1. The life of Eugene Meyer.
2. The life of Katherine Meyer Graham.
3. The Federal Reserve Board.
4. The early history of the *Washington Post*.

Katharine Meyer Graham (1917-   ) is the daughter of Eugene Meyer, a self-made millionaire who was once chairman of the Federal Reserve Board[1]. When the *Washington Post* was auctioned in 1933, Meyer was the mysterious stranger who bid it in for a bargain $825,000. [...]

As a young woman, Katharine feared she would never be able to live up to the standards of her family. During and after her college years, she worked as a reporter on the *San Francisco News* as well as on her father's *Washington Post*. In 1940 she retired, without regrets, to marry Phil Graham, a young lawyer. [...]

After the war, Eugene Meyer persuaded Graham to join the *Post* as publisher, and in 1948, he sold the voting stock of the paper to the Grahams on their promise to continue its tradition of "virile, strong, and independent concern for the general welfare". Meyer and Graham were a good business team, and they set out to acquire properties. They bought the Washington *Times Herald*, *Newsweek* Magazine, radio and television stations, and a news service.

Then the catastrophe struck which jolted Katharine out of her comfortable life as a Washington matron. Phil Graham suffered increasingly more serious manic-depressive cycles. In 1963 he shot himself to death, leaving Katharine a publishing empire worth hundreds of millions of dollars. She could have sold it, but she had promised her father that she would maintain the *Post*'s tradition of public service. Someone had to take Phil Graham's place, and Katharine nominated herself. [...]

The *Post* thrived under Katharine's management. James Reston, an editor of the *New York Times* and former chief of its Washington bureau, thought it became "an immensely better paper than it was when she took it over". Word spread that Katharine was becoming a power, but she resisted the compliment. [...] She worked hard to escape notice, ducking interviewers, and using her knowledge of journalism to keep herself out of the papers. People in Washington knew about her, but she was not a national figure.

She gave others the credit but she took the risks herself. It was her decision, in 1971, to publish the controversial Pentagon Papers and thus expose the *Post* to reprisals, if not court action, for printing classified material illegally "leaked" or stolen from a government office.

Then came the Watergate scandal. It broke as a local story in the *Post* — a local story that only an alert newsroom would have pursued. Katharine did not interfere or direct, but she followed the story every day. "My role was to make sure we were being fair and we were being factual and we were being accurate," she says. "I had to ask every question I could think of because the reputation of the paper was clearly at stake." [...]

Offices of the *Washington Post*.

Kay Graham has become noticeably more feminist. In 1970, for instance she refused to attend the all-male Gridiron Club[2] dinner because women less important than herself were not invited on the same basis as men. She had quietly contributed $20,000 to help found *Ms*[3] Magazine, but it was not until a few years later that she spoke on behalf of the magazine in public.

Kay Graham is personally modest. [...] She credits the unraveling of Watergate to her staff, to the press in general, to the courts, to Congress — to anyone but herself. But it is increasingly difficult even for her to maintain that she deserves no personal credit for what she has done because she fell into her position, as she once put it, "by matrimony and patrimony". Women who inherit large-scale enterprises do not usually undertake to run them personally. For the brilliant performance of the *Washington Post,* Katharine Graham must take some credit herself.

Caroline Bird: *Enterprising Women*

1. Federal Reserve Board: the Board regulating the U.S. banking system. 2. Gridiron: field for American football. 3. Ms.: used as an address for all women married or not.

B. UNDERSTANDING VOCABULARY IN CONTEXT. Circle the correct answer.

1. When the *Washington Post* was _____ in 1933, Meyer was the man who bid it in for a bargain. (paragraph 1)

   a. closed
   b. sold

2. As a young woman, Katherine feared she would never be able to _____. (paragraph 2)

   a. make as much money as her father.
   b. do as well as her family expected her to do.

3. In 1940 she retired _____ to marry Phil Graham. (paragraph 2)

   a. happily
   b. unhappily

4. Phil Graham suffered increasingly more serious _____ problems. (**paragraph 4**)

   a. physical
   b. psychological

5. The *Post* was _____ under Katherine's management. (paragraph 5)

   a. very successful
   b. not very successful

6. Katherine Graham _____ interviews. (paragraph 5)

   a. gave
   b. didn't give

7. It was her decision to publish the Pentagon Papers and expose the *Post* to reprisals _____ court action. (paragraph 6)

   a. and maybe
   b. but not

8. Ms. Graham said that reporting on the Watergate scandal had to be done very carefully because the *Post* could be _____ . (paragraph 7)

   a. ruined.
   b. even more successful.

9. Ms. Graham spoke _____ *Ms. Magazine* in public. (paragraph 8)

   a. in favor of
   b. against

10. Ms. Graham credits everyone but herself for _____ the Watergate scandal. (paragraph 9)

   a. uncovering
   b. ignoring

C. DISCUSSION. To what extent is Katherine Graham typical of a woman living in today's world?

FROM GADGETS TO PEOPLE

America's genius with high technology may have put men on the moon, but there is growing skepticism about its ability to solve human problems closer to home.

In fact, a subtle but significant shift from purely technological solutions is already under way as scientists argue openly for new directions in research.

A growing number of scientists insist that answers to the world's problems will not come from a flashier array of electronics and machines. Instead, as they see it, solutions must evolve from a better understanding of the humans that drive the system and from a fuller appreciation of the limits and potential of the earth's resources.

What this means is an increased emphasis on the life and earth sciences, on sociology, psychology, economics and even philosophy. [...]

More and more of the best minds in science, particularly young researchers, are being drawn into these developing fields. [...]

Industry officials are concerned by a declining rate of innovation in technology. Patent applications by Americans have been dropping in the U.S. since 1971. Yet many scientists seem to be saying: The need for better televisions, bigger power plants and faster airplanes — markers of rapid-fire technological creativity — is becoming marginal at best. The market in the industrialized nations for this kind of technology, it is claimed, is reaching a saturation point. [...]

All this is not to say that technological creativity will not play a critical role in solving energy and food shortages, or that answers to environmental difficulties will not come from further advances in the same technologies that may have helped cause the problems.

Where the real challenge lies, in the view of the new breed of scientists, is in finding ways to produce goods to meet the world's needs, using less of the raw materials that are becoming scarce. [...]

Roger Revelle, a Harvard professor and authority on global food and population problems, maintains that greater efforts to understand all living systems, particularly human beings, must be given a higher priority in the research community.

Mr Revelle, who traveled recently in India and Nepal, points out that America's high technology often has little use when transferred to less-developed nations. Elaborate machinery that works well for an Iowa farmer can be useless for most people who till the soil in India.

What the Indian farmer needs is some innovative "low" technology — for example, a better one-piece plow that can be pulled by a water buffalo.

In the United States many high-technology companies are increasingly reluctant to pursue new twists in research until they have assurances that the experimental work will result in near-term profits.

More and more of industry's research money is going toward improving existing products and toward defending those already on the market against charges that they use too much energy, pollute or pose some other safety hazard to the worker and consumer.

From *U.S. News & World Report*,
Nov. 8, 1976

Why are these people protesting?

A. RECOGNIZING POINTS OF VIEW. This article lists several challenges that many American scientists feel must be met so that technology can be used to solve human problems. According to these scientists, what should be done? Check the correct answers.

_____ **1.** Try to understand human resources better.

_____ **2.** Design more complex machines and electronic equipment.

_____ **3.** Understand the limits of natural resources.

_____ **4.** Emphasize social and biological sciences.

_____ **5.** Encourage more patent applications.

_____ **6.** Encourage rapid-fire technological creativity such as bigger power plants.

_____ **7.** Solve energy and food shortages.

_____ **8.** Develop synthetic energy sources.

_____ **9.** Find ways to produce needed goods using fewer raw materials.

_____ **10.** Look for innovative ''low'' technology.

_____ **11.** Improve existing products.

_____ **12.** Defend products on the market from charges that they use too much energy, pollute or pose a safety hazard.

B. DISCUSSION. What do you think is the most urgent technological problem to be solved today?

Space Hardware Comes to Earth

The space program was developed to probe the mysteries of the solar system, but it has also contributed to numerous technological improvements here at home.

Take a look at this list of only a few of the secondary applications of aerospace technology:

• Skylab carbon monoxide monitor is currently being used to measure monoxide pollution in urban areas.

• Viking dirt analyzer can help identify poisons in humans by analyzing the patient's blood.

• Heated space suit technology has led to heated protective clothing (boots, gloves, caps) used by construction workers and consumers.

• Control switch developed so immobilized astronauts could operate controls by eye motion now makes it possible for paralyzed patients to control television, book page turner, bed position, lights and other objects.

• Aircraft icing research information was used to reduce ice build up in commercial planes.

• Miniature Viking seismometer and its computer could help predict quakes on earth.

• Rubber tire with low temperature pliability developed for Apollo-14 mission has led to a studless winter automobile tire that provides traction equal to or better than studded tires on slick surfaces. This is especially important in states that are banning studded tires due to poor traction on dry surfaces and destruction of roads.

• Horizontal shower developed for use in long-term bedrest studies related to lengthy space missions can now be used for bathing bedridden patients. Unit consists of horizontal water-tight compartment with multiple shower heads.

The most important and lasting impact of the entire space effort, however, is in the field of education. NASA has played a key role in developing source materials for teaching space-oriented mathematics. ◆

A. UNDERSTANDING VOCABULARY IN CONTEXT. Circle the correct answer.

1. The *Skylab carbon monoxide monitor* (paragraph 3) is probably
   a. something that shows the amount of carbon monoxide in the air inside the Skylab.
   b. something that shows the amount of carbon monoxide in the atmosphere.
   c. something that uses carbon monoxide to monitor inside the Skylab.

2. The *Viking dirt analyzer* (paragraph 4) is probably
   a. made of dirt.
   b. the specialist who analyzes the dirt found in the Viking.
   c. something that analyzes dirt.

3. *Heated space suit technology has led to heated protective clothing* (paragraph 5) to
   a. keep people warm.
   b. provide consumers with space clothes.
   c. protect people from accidents.

4. *Immobilized* astronauts and *paralyzed* patients (paragraph 6)
   a. are sick.
   b. do things with their bodies.
   c. do things with their eyes.

B. DISCUSSION. How can we justify spending money on aerospace technology when there are so many unresolved problems here on earth?

Roots

In Roots *Alex Haley traces back six generations of black Americans directly to the original African ancestor who was kidnapped one day when he went out to cut wood for a new drum. In this passage Haley's newly-freed great-grandparents decide to leave the plantation where they had been slaves until the Emancipation Proclamation freed them.*

In pindrop quiet and with his born sense of drama, Chicken George told them that he had found for them all a western Tennessee settlement whose white people anxiously awaited their arrival to help build a town. [...]

The family never let him finish in their wild excitement. As some went dashing off to boast to others on adjacent plantations, Tom began planning that afternoon how to alter a farm wagon into a covered "Rockaway[1]", of which about ten could move all of the units of the family to this new place. But by that sundown a dozen other hands of newly freed families had come — not asking, but demanding that their families, too, were going. [...]

Amid the next two months of feverish activity, the men built the "Rockaways". The women butchered, cooked, canned, and smoked foodstuffs for travel and selected what other vital things to take. Old Chicken George strode about, supervising every activity, loving his hero role. Tom Murray was thronged with volunteered assistance from yet more newly freed families, and with assurances that they would swiftly obtain their own wagons to become their family's "Rockaways". Finally he announced that all who wished could go — but that there must be but one "Rockaway" per family unit. When at last twenty-eight wagons were packed and ready to roll on the following sunup, in a strange calm sense of sadness, the freed people went about gently touching the familiar things, washpots, the fenceposts, knowing that it was for the last time. [...]

Tom Murray had retired for the night within his wagon when he heard the light knocking at the tailgate[2]. Somehow he knew who was there even before he opened the end flap. Ol' George Johnson stood there, his face working with emotion, his hands wringing his hat. "Tom — like a word with you, if you got time —."

Climbing down from the wagon, Tom Murray followed Ol' George Johnson off a way in the moonlight. When finally Ol' George stopped, he was so choked with embarrassment and emotion that he could hardly talk. "Me and Martha been talkin' [...] Tom, we been wonderin' if y'all[3] let us go along where you goin'?"

It was awhile before Tom spoke. "If it was jes'[4] my family, I could tell you right now. [...] I let you know —."

Tom went to each other wagon, knocking gently, calling out the men. Gathering them, he told them what happened. [...]

There was sharp opposition from some, some of it antiwhite. But after a while someone spoke quietly, "He can't help it if he white —." Finally, a vote was taken, and a majority said that the Johnsons could go.

Alex Haley: *Roots,* 1976

---

1. rockaway: a covered wagon like those of pioneers.   **2.** tailgate: the back-end of a vehicle (cf. here, the end-flap).   **3.** y'all: you all, or you.   **4.** jes': just.

A. INFERRING MEANING. Circle the correct answer.

1. The ceremonial head of the family was probably

   a. Chicken George.
   b. Tom.

2. The administrative head of the family was probably

   a. Chicken George.
   b. Tom.

3. Ol' George Johnson was probably

   a. a slave owner.
   b. someone who worked for a slave owner.
   c. another slave.

4. George Johnson was

   a. afraid he wouldn't be able to go to Tennessee.
   b. pretty sure that he would be able to go to Tennessee.

5. In the family the _____ made the important decisions.

   a. men
   b. women

B. DISCUSSION. Do you think the Johnsons should have been allowed to go?

A rare old photograph of actual slaves on a cotton plantation in the South more than a hundred years ago.

"We've come a long way, babe!"

"Like most black Americans, my roots are in the South." So writes Time's *Atlanta correspondent, Jack White, 30. Here is his personal account of being brought up under segregation.*

My father's father was born a slave somewhere near Savannah, Ga. My mother's father was the son of a white undertaker and his mulatto concubine in a small town in
5 North Carolina.

Like many other blacks, my parents migrated North to find education and better opportunities. My father went to Howard University[1] medical school, and my mother
10 went to Howard's nursing school. My parents wanted to shelter their children from segregation and all its belittling aspects, so they settled in Washington, which turned out to be as segregated a city as one could find.

15 **Segregated echo.** In the 1950s, a clerk in a department store refused to let me sip from a water fountain, despite my mother's plea that "he's just a little boy". Later, when my family got its first television set, I was
20 entranced by the ads for Glen Echo amusement park. My mother couldn't really explain why she couldn't take me there. The reason, of course, was that Glen Echo did not admit blacks. Nor did many restaurants,
25 movie theaters and other public facilities.

My deepest realization of what the Old South was really like came in about 1962, when my father, brother, a friend and I drove South to my grandmother's house in Stuart,
30 Fla. On the way we were denied a room in a Holiday Inn in Savannah, and wound up sleeping in a "rooming house" (read whorehouse) that hadn't had an overnight guest in years. In Stuart, my father went into
35 a hardware store to buy a Thermos bottle. The white clerk asked my dad, a distinguished professor of surgery at least 20 years his senior, "What you want, boy?" My father struggled to maintain his dignity as he told
40 the clerk what he wanted. I felt in my gut, for the first time, how hard it had been for black men to preserve their self-respect under a rigid system of white supremacy.

Southern pride. Because of the civil rights
45 movement, I will never have to explain to my four-year-old son that he can't go to an amusement park or swim in a public swimming pool just because he is black. He will never see me diminish in his eyes because
50 some white man can lord it over me and make me seem like a child.

White Southerners are now taking a great deal of pride in the region's rapid adjustment to the post-civil rights era. The fact is that
55 every change was resisted, every improvement fought, every overture turned back. Though many Southerners were made uneasy by the oppressive pattern of Southern race relations, most did little or nothing to
60 change it. [...] Without unrelenting pressure from blacks and the Federal Government, white Southerners would never have changed. Southern behavior has changed, but the hearts, for the most part, are
65 probably just the same.

White Southerners tend to have a passion for lost causes. The Washington Redskins, for example, were the South's "adopted" pro-football team. They remained lily-white,
70 and they retained their Southern constituency, even though they were consistent losers. [...] The Redskins' ownership would rather be white than winners.

Then the team's owner, George Preston
75 Marshall, died, and Lawyer Edward Bennett Williams took over. Williams realized that he was in a new day, and the Redskins began to get black players. Within a few years, they became winners. Now everybody loves them.

80 Much the same thing has happened to the South. It has become a region of winners. Blacks are playing on the team. Points are going on the scoreboard. But is the change permanent?

85 My own guess is that the good impulses will win out. The Southern white man, even at his most bigoted, always had some noble impulses: loyalty, independence, courage. Martin Luther King spoke of the "redemp-
90 tive power" of nonviolent love, and his followers nodded amen. They believed white Southerners could be redeemed. And if they thought that, after 350 years of oppression, who am I to quarrel?

From *Time*, Sept 27, 1976

---

1. Howard University: prestigious black university in Washington D.C.

A graduating class at Howard University.

A. UNDERSTANDING VOCABULARY IN CONTEXT. Circle the best paraphrase.

1. *My parents wanted to shelter their children from segregation* (lines 10–12) means

    a. my parents wanted their children to know what segregation was like.
    b. my parents didn't want their children to know what segregation was like.

2. *Segregation and all its belittling aspects* (lines 11–12) means

    a. segregation and its negative aspects.
    b. segregation and its few aspects.

3. *I was entranced* (line 20) means

    a. I was very excited and curious.
    b. I was afraid.

4. *We . . . wound up sleeping in a "rooming house"* (lines 30–32) means

    a. we refused to sleep in a rooming house.
    b. we slept in a rooming house.

5. *My father struggled to maintain his dignity* (lines 38–39) means

    a. he got into a fight with the clerk.
    b. he remained calm.

6. *Lord it over me* (line 50) means

   a. act superior to me.
   b. pray for me.

7. *Unrelenting pressure* (line 60) means

   a. pressure sometimes.
   b. pressure·all the time.

8. *Consistent losers* (lines 71–72) means

   a. losers sometimes.
   b. losers all the time.

9. *Even at his most bigoted* (lines 86–87) means

   a. even at his best.
   b. even at his worst.

B. UNDERSTANDING THE USE OF QUOTATION MARKS. Circle the correct answer.

1. ''*Rooming house*'' (line 32) has quotation marks because

   a. it is the title of a book.
   b. that is exactly what the sign on the house says.
   c. it really isn't a rooming house, but a house of prostitution.

2. ''*Adopted*'' (line 68) has quotation marks because

   a. *adopted* usually means that a husband and wife take a child that isn't their own into their family.
   b. the Washington Redskins weren't very popular in the South.
   c. Washington isn't really in the South.

C. INFERRING MEANING. Circle the correct answer.

1. Jack White's parents _____ Washington to be a segregated city. (lines 10–14)

   a. expected
   b. did not expect

2. In the '50s in the South black people _____ use the same water fountains as white people. (lines 15–18)

   a. could
   b. ~~could~~ not

   ~~did~~ the clerk call White's father *boy*? (line 38)

   ~~is~~ the customary way for clerks to address their customers.
   ~~is~~ an insulting term that white men often used when talking to black men.

   74–79 describe

   ~~the~~ social situation in the South.
   ~~S~~outhern football team.

5. The author thinks (lines 85–94)

    a. the South will return to segregation in the future.

    b. the South will not return to segregation in the future.

D. DISCUSSION

1. What do you think makes people racist?

2. In what way do you think the writer shares in the American Dream?

[handwritten: 1619 First slave shipment to New World]

FACTS AND DATA ON BLACK AMERICANS

1820
Slavery permitted only south of the Mason-Dixon line (36° 40N) in "Dixie."

1861–1865
Civil War

[handwritten: 1863 – Emanc. Proc.]

After the Civil War
Congress creates Freedman's Bureau to assist former slaves (1865–1872).
Ku Klux Klan founded (1866).
Atlanta and Howard Universities, admitting men and women of all races, founded (1865 and 1867).
Reconstruction Acts passed (1867 and 1868).
Fourteenth (Civil Rights) and Fifteenth (Negro Suffrage) Amendments ratified (1868 and 1870).

1909
National Association for the Advancement of Colored People (NAACP) founded to eliminate racial injustice.

After World War I
Drift of black population from southern states toward industrial centers in the Northeast.

1926
Arturo Schomburg's collection of literature and art documenting Afro-American history incorporated into the New York City Public Library.

1954
Supreme Court decision in *Brown v. Board of Education of Topeka* prohibits segregation in tax-supported schools, universities and places of recreation.

1955
Supreme Court decision in *Brown II* specifies that the responsibility for desegregation lies chiefly with local school authorities and that it be done with "all deliberate speed."

1957
Southern Christian Leadership Conference (SCLC) organized, headed by Martin Luther King, Jr.

1960–1975
Black Pride Movement: return to African cultural traditions encouraged by Black Muslims, Malcolm X and other separatists. Black Studies become part of college and high school curricula.

1963
Civil Rights March on Washington attended by an estimated 250,000 people.

1964
Civil Rights Acts passed abolishing all forms of segregation and securing political rights. Vast welfare program for Blacks initiated.

1965–1975
Dramatic increase in number of Black officeholders and voters in both North and South.
Shirley Anita St. Hill Chisholm, New York State Congresswoman: first Black woman elected to Congress.
Thurgood Marshall, U.S. Supreme Court Justice: first Black appointed to U.S. Supreme Court.
Robert Clifton Weaver, Former Secretary of Department of Housing and Urban Development: first Black member of Presidential Cabinet.
Andrew Young, Former U.S. Ambassador to the United Nations: first Black appointed to this post.

1970–present
Explosive growth of popular entertainment and the arts, featuring Black performers and Black thematic material.

[handwritten: 1995 – Simpson trial]
[handwritten: 1995 – Mississippi officially accepts the 14th Amendment]

What do you think these women mean by the American Dream? Do you agree that it is for men only?

Carol

By the time Carol was twenty-six she was making a lot of money for a girl her age, and she had quit her job to write full time. [...] All her friends from high school had married and she had been a bridesmaid several times. Her college friends had married too, but she did not see them anymore because the ones she liked did not live in New York. She now had her name on magazine covers occasionally, and she   5
had a certain following and received fan letters, some of them from men proposing marriage. She wrote a piece on lonely people who wrote love letters to strangers. It was the first piece she had written with heart, and afterward she had to have her telephone number unlisted.

Her mother and her mother's friends viewed her rising career with dismay. Her   10
mother said, "Boys don't want to marry girls who are too independent".

Because everyone she met at parties talked about their analysis, Carol treated herself to a year of analysis to find out why she had never married. [...] The doctor was just a man to her, she couldn't think of him as a doctor or an authority, although once when she had a sore throat she asked him to look at it since she was paying him   15
anyway, and he prescribed some pills. She was aware that he thought she was funny and interesting because he laughed a lot at the things she said. She also became aware after a few months that he didn't think she was sick, or at least what he considered her sickness was that she did not fit into the role he saw for her as a young woman.   20
— "You are lonely," he said. "I would like to see you married. You would be a wonderful mother."

— "But I really don't feel I'm ready for that. There are so many things I haven't done yet."

— "You're lucky you can write. You can stay at home with the children and write." 25

— "Only if they're zombies," she said.

— "You could marry a rich man. You could have a nurse for the children."

— "Then why have them? If I had kids I'd want to enjoy being with them."

— "Your parents must have made you feel very unwanted," he said sadly.

— "Unwanted? They never let me out of their sight." 30

— "You must understand you are rejecting being feminine."

— "If being feminine means washing some guy's socks, then how come every Chinese laundryman down on the corner doesn't feel his masculinity threatened?"

— "You retreat into words," he said.

— "That's how I express myself." 35

— "You could express yourself as a woman if you had a man to take care of you."

— "Then how come I don't fall in love?" Carol asked. [...] "I'd get married if I could find somebody I really loved."

— "There have been cases where love came afterward."

— "You mean a marriage of convenience?" she said, horrified. 40

— "It has worked."

— Not for me, she thought. "Do you think I'm really neurotic?" she asked.

— "The only area in which you function perfectly is your work. In the human area you need more work here."

She could see herself trotting obediently off to the analyst twice a week until she got 45
married, and then still "more work" at the analyst until she produced two children,
a number the doctor found ideal for mental health, and then more sessions of
"work" until she was safely living in the suburbs. It could take years!

Rona Jaffe: *The Other Woman*

A. **UNDERSTANDING VOCABULARY IN CONTEXT/DISCUSSION.** You might
not understand the meaning of some of the words or expressions that you just read.
Work in groups and try to figure out the meaning of these words using other information
from the reading or your own experience.

fan letters (line 6)
dismay (line 10)
zombies (line 26)
marriage of convenience (line 40)
horrified (line 40)
neurotic (line 42)

B. INTERPRETING LANGUAGE. Circle the correct answer.

1. When Carol's mother says, ''Boys don't want to marry girls who are too independent'' (line 11), she is probably

   a. explaining to her friends why Carol isn't married.
   b. talking to Carol and criticizing her because she isn't married.

2. When Carol says, ''Only if they're zombies'' (line 26), she is saying

   a. she wants her children not to bother her so that she can continue writing.
   b. she won't have much time to write because children are active and must be cared for.

3. When Carol says, ''They never let me out of their sight'' (line 30), she is

   a. criticizing her parents.
   b. disagreeing with her doctor's opinion.

4. When the doctor says, ''You retreat into words'' (line 34), he is

   a. criticizing Carol.
   b. complimenting Carol.

5. When the doctor says, ''There have been cases where love came afterward'' (line 39), he is

   a. telling Carol about some of his other patients.
   b. suggesting to Carol that she might get married even if she isn't in love.

C. DISCUSSION

1. The analyst says, ''You could express yourself as a woman if you had a man to take care of you.'' What do you think? Is Carol expressing herself as a woman now? Does she need a man to take care of her?

2. Do you think that the American Dream is for men only? Why or why not?

3. In what way do you think Carol reflects the American Dream?

D. DEBATE

These are accurate descriptions of men and women.

THE FINISHED PRODUCT

Mr. Media	Mrs. Media
Tall, dark handsome working model	36-25-36 blond model
Guaranteed indefinitely, improves with age	Guaranteed approximately 25 years
Power driven	Runs cheaply on love
Where would you be without him?	Every home should have one!
An essential item	An attractive decoration
A life-long investment	A bargain at any price

WOMEN IN PROFESSIONAL AND MANAGERIAL POSITIONS

YEAR	PROFESSIONAL AND TECHNICAL WORKERS	MANAGERS AND ADMINISTRATORS EXCLUDING FARM
1900	434,000	74,000
1950	1,794,000	990,000
1960	2,703,000	1,099,000
1970	4,298,000	1,321,000
1975	5,665,000	1,725,000
1980	6,917,000	2,850,000
1981 (Sept.)	7,187,000	3,083,000

Source: U.S. Dept. of Labor Statistics, Employment and Earnings

" *Welcome aboard. This is your captain, Margaret Williamson, speaking.* "

Drawing by Richter; ©1973. The New Yorker Magazine, Inc.

III.
The Other Side of the Dream

HOW THE INDIANS SAW IT

For many people and for a long time, "a good Indian [was] a dead Indian," and the pain of the Indian as he experienced the death of his way of life was simply not understood. Yet on many occasions Indian people tried to explain their feelings to the white man. Here are a few passages from speeches or interviews in which the Indians speak for themselves.

Ma-ka-tai-ma-she-kia-kiak or Black Hawk, Chief of the Sauk and Fox[1], in 1833 :

We always had plenty; our children never cried from hunger, neither were our people in want... The rapids of Rock River furnished us with an abundance of excellent fish, and the land being very fertile never failed to produce good crops of corn, beans, pumpkins, and squashes... Here our village stood for more than a hundred years, during all of which time we were the undisputed possessors of the Mississippi Valley... Our village was healthy and there was no place in the country possessing such advantages, nor hunting grounds better than those we had in possession. If a prophet had come to our village and told us that the things were to take place which have since come to pass, none of our people would have believed him.

Chief Luther Standing Bear[2], of the Oglala[3] band of Sioux[4], in the 1930s :

We did not think of the great open plains, the beautiful rolling hills, and winding streams with tangled growth, as "wild". Only to the white man was nature a "wilderness" and only to him was the land "infested" with "wild" animals and "savage" people. To us it was tame. Earth was bountiful and we were surrounded with the blessings of the Great Mystery. Not until the hairy man from the east came and with brutal frenzy heaped injustices upon us and the families we loved was it "wild" for us. When the very animals of the forest began fleeing from his approach, then it was that for us the "Wild West" began.

An old Wintu[5] Woman, in the 1950s :

The white people never cared for land or deer or bear. When we Indians kill meat, we eat it all up. When we dig roots, we make little holes. When we build houses, we make ———— n we burn grass for grasshoppers, we don't ruin things. We shake down ——nuts. We don't chop down the trees. We only use dead wood. But the —w up the ground, pull down the trees, kill everything. The tree says, —. Don't hurt me." But they chop it down and cut it up. The spirit of the —— They blast out trees and stir it up to its depths. They saw up the trees. —— The Indians never hurt anything, but the white people destroy all. They —catter them on the ground. The rock says, "Don't. You are hurting me." —ple pay no attention. When the Indians use rocks, they take little round —king... How can the spirit of the earth like the white man ?... Everywhere —as touched it, it is sore.

47

Aleek-chea-ahoosh or Plenty Coups, a Crow[6] chief,
in his autobiography,
published before his death in 1932 :

By the time I was forty I could see our country was changing fast and that these changes were causing us to live very differently. Anybody could now see that soon there would be no buffalo on the plains, and everybody was wondering how we could live after they were gone. There were few war parties and almost no raids... White men with their spotted buffalo were on the plains about us. Their houses were near the water holes, and their villages on the rivers. We made up our minds to be friendly with them, in spite of all the changes they were bringing. But we found this difficult, because the white men too often promised to do one thing and then when they acted at all, did another.

T.C. McLuhan : *Touch the Earth*

---

1. Sauk and Fox: a tribe of Indians of the Wisconsin area. **2.** Luther Standing Bear: an example of the christianization of Indian culture. **3.** Ogala: a tribe of Sioux inhabiting the Teton area. **4.** Sioux: a generic name for a series of tribes inhabiting the Plains west of the Mississippi. **5.** Wintu: a people of the Sacramento Valley, California. **6.** Crow: a tribe of the Sioux inhabiting the region between the Platte and Yellowstone rivers.

North American Indian digging roots.

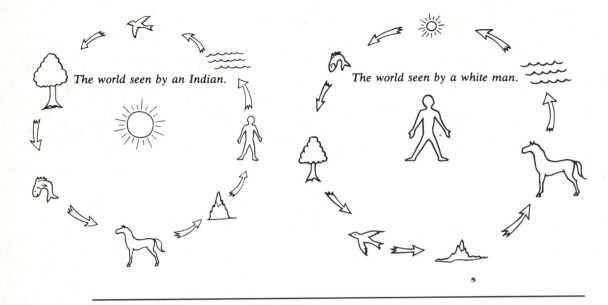

The world seen by an Indian.

The world seen by a white man.

A. LOCATING SPECIFIC INFORMATION. Fill in the correct information.

1. What are the three reasons Chief Black Hawk gives for why they *always had plenty; (our) children never cried from hunger*? _____

_____

2. In describing the white man's view of the land, Chief Luther Standing Bear uses some words that leave a negative impression and give the idea that the land was an unpleasant place to live. What are these words?

_____

3. What are the positive words he uses to describe the Indians' view of nature?

_____

4. What examples does the Wintu Woman give to describe how the Indians take care of the land? _____

_____

5. What examples does she give to describe how the white men hurt the land?

_____

_____

6. What examples does Chief Plenty Coups give to describe how the country was ⸮ging? _____

_____

SION. In view of present environmental problems, what lessons could the ⸮n learn from the Indian?

_____

Greer County[1] Bachelor

The various "homestead acts" that were passed throughout the 19th century gave anyone who was willing to bring it into cultivation the possibility of getting a piece of land from the government at a very low price. Pioneers were encouraged to settle always further West, but they apparently were not all too happy about their "government claims", as this anonymous ballad suggests.

My name is Tom High, an old bachelor am I,
You'll find me out West in the county of fame,
You'll find me out West on an elegant plain,
A-starving to death on my government claim.

My clothes they are ragged, my language is rough,
My bread is corndodgers, both solid and tough;
And yet I am happy and live at my ease,
On sorghum, molasses, and bacon and cheese.

Hurrah for Greer county, the land of the free,
The land of the bedbug, grasshopper and flea,
I'll sing of its praise, I'll tell of its fame,
While starving to death on my government claim.

Hurrah for Greer county where blizzards arise,
Where the sun never sinks and the flea never dies.
I'll sing of its praises, I'll tell of its fame,
While starving to death on my government claim.

My house it is built of the national soil,
Its walls are erected according to Hoyle[2],
Its roof has no pitch but is level and plain,
I always get wet if it happens to rain.

How happy I am when I crawl into bed,
A rattlesnake hisses a tune at my head,
A grey little centipede, quite without fear,
Crawls over my pillow and into my ear.

Now all you claim holders, I hope you'll stay,
Chew your hardtack till you're toothless and grey,
But for myself, I'll no longer remain,
To starve like a dog on my government claim.

Good-bye to Greer county, good-bye to the West,
I'll travel back East to the girl I love best.
I'll travel back East and marry me a wife,
Call quits on corndodgers for the rest of my life.

anon

---

1. Greer County: county in Oklahoma. **2.** Hoyle: a writer on card games; a house built according to Hoyle: a house of cards.

A. **UNDERSTANDING VOCABULARY IN CONTEXT.** Fill in the blanks.

1. Find the phrase in stanza 1 that means ''not having enough to eat.'' _____

_____

2. Find the phrase in stanza 1 that means ''the land given by the government.'' _____

_____

3. Find the word in stanza 2 that shows that his clothes don't look very good. _____

_____

4. Find three examples of insects in stanza 3. _____

_____

5. Find an example of bad weather in stanza 4. _____

6. Find two words in stanza 7 that might describe an old person. _____

_____

7. Find a phrase in the last stanza that means ''give up.'' _____

B. **RECOGNIZING IRONY.** The author gives an accurate description of his life in some lines while using irony in others. Check the lines that are ironic.

_____ 1. *You'll find me out West on an elegant plain.*

_____ 2. *My clothes they are ragged, my language is rough.*

_____ 3. *And yet I am happy and live at my ease.*

_____ 4. *Hurrah for Greer county where blizzards arise.*

_____ 5. *I always get wet if it happens to rain.*

_____ 6. *How happy I am when I crawl into bed.*

_____ 7. *I'll travel back East to the girl I love best.*

C. **COMPOSITION.** Write a letter as Tom High describing your life to a friend who would like to apply for a government claim.

D. **DISCUSSION.** In what way does this ballad clash with the popular view of the conquest of the West?

Immigrants arriving in New York at the beginning of the century.

1902 : They Came to America

In Ragtime, *E.L. Doctorow draws the portrait of the U.S. in the first years of the 20th century. A series of loose sketches, the novel is tied together by the presence in different episodes of the same characters, among whom is a family of Jewish immigrants from Eastern Europe, who appear under the names of Mameh and Tateh, as their young daughter calls them.*

Most of the immigrants came from Italy and Eastern Europe. They were taken in launches to Ellis Island[1]. There, in a curiously ornate human warehouse of red brick and gray stone, they were tagged, given showers and arranged on benches in waiting pens. They were immediately sensitive to the enormous power of the immigration officials. These officials changed names they couldn't pronounce and   5
tore people from their families, consigning to a return voyage old folks, people with bad eyes, riffraff and also those who looked insolent. Such power was dazzling. The immigrants were reminded of home. They went into the streets and were somehow absorbed in the tenements. They were despised by New Yorkers. They were filthy and illiterate. They stank of fish and garlic. They had running sores. They had no   10
honor and worked for next to nothing. They stole. They drank. They raped their own daughters. They killed each other casually. Among those who despised them the most were the second-generation Irish, whose fathers had been guilty of the same crimes. Irish kids pulled the beards of old Jews and knocked them down. They upended the pushcarts of Italian peddlers.   15

Every season of the year wagons came through the streets and picked up bodies of derelicts. Late at night old ladies in babushkas[2] came to the morgue looking for their husbands and sons. The corpses lay on tables of galvanized iron. From the bottom of each table a drainpipe extended to the floor. Around the rim of the table was a culvert. And into the culvert ran the water sprayed constantly over each   20
body from an overhead faucet. The faces of the dead were upturned into the streams of water that poured over them like the irrepressible mechanism in death of their own tears.

But somehow piano lessons began to be heard. People stitched themselves to the flag. They carved paving stones for the streets. They sang. They told jokes. The   25
family lived in one room and everyone worked: Mameh and the little girl sewed knee pants and got seventy cents a dozen. They sewed from the time they got up to the time they went to bed. Tateh made his living in the street. As time went on they got to know the city. One Sunday, in a wild impractical mood, they spent twelve cents for three fares on the streetcar and rode uptown. They walked on Madison   30
Avenue and Fifth Avenue and looked at the mansions. Their owners called them palaces. And that's what they were, they were palaces. [...] Tateh was a socialist. He looked at the palaces and his heart was outraged. The family walked quickly. The police in their tall helmets looked at them. On these wide empty sidewalks in this part of the city the police did not like to see immigrants. [...]   35
A crisis came to the family when somebody delivered a letter telling them the little girl would have to go to school. This meant they could not make ends meet. Helplessly, Mameh and Tateh took their child to the school. She was enrolled and went off each day. Tateh roamed the streets. He didn't know what to do. He had a peddler's business. Never could he find a place at the curb that was profitable.   40
While he was gone Mameh sat by the window with her stack of cut cloth and pedaled the sewing machine. She was a petite dark-eyed woman with wavy brown hair which she parted in the middle and tied behind her neck in a bun. When she was alone like this she sang softly to herself in a high sweet thin voice. Her songs had no words. One afternoon she took her finished work to the loft on Stanton Street. The owner   45
invited her into his office. He looked at the piece goods carefully and said she had done well. He counted out the money, adding a dollar more than she deserved. This he explained was because she was such a good-looking woman. He smiled. He touched Mameh's breast. Mameh fled, taking the dollar. The next time the same thing happened. She told Tateh she was doing more work. She became accustomed   50
to the hands of her employer. One day with two weeks' rent due she let the man have his way on a cutting table. He kissed her face and tasted the salt of her tears.

E.L. Doctorow: *Ragtime*

---

1. Ellis Island: an island in New York bay for quarantining immigrants. 2. babushkas: headscarves as worn by Russian women.

A. UNDERSTANDING VOCABULARY IN CONTEXT/DISCUSSION. You might not understand the meaning of some of the words or expressions that you just read. Work in groups and try to figure out the meaning of these words using other information from the reading or your own experience.

despised (line 9)
sewed (line 26)
mansions (line 31)
outraged (line 33)
make ends meet (line 37)

B. LOCATING SPECIFIC INFORMATION. Check the correct answers.

1. What are examples of the dehumanizing treatment the immigrants received?

_____ **a.** They were tagged.

_____ **b.** They had to put on new clothes.

_____ **c.** They were put on benches in waiting pens.

_____ **d.** The officials changed names they couldn't pronounce.

_____ **e.** Families were separated.

_____ **f.** Unmarried women were sent home.

_____ **g.** Old people were sent home.

_____ **h.** People who didn't have any money were sent home.

_____ **i.** People who looked like they might cause trouble were sent home.

2. What did the New Yorkers think of the new immigrants?

_____ **a.** They were lazy.

_____ **b.** They were dirty.

_____ **c.** They smelled bad.

_____ **d.** They were too timid.

_____ **e.** They didn't speak English well.

_____ **f.** They stole.

_____ **g.** They were very violent.

C. INFERRING MEANING. Circle the correct answer.

1. According to paragraph 1, the immigrants were reminded of home when

   a. they felt the power of the immigration officials.
   b. they had to say goodbye to the people who were sent back home.

2. In line 14 _old Jews_ are

   a. new immigrants.
   b. second-generation immigrants.

3. In lines 21–23 it says that _streams of water_

   a. couldn't be turned off.
   b. looked like human tears.

4. _People stitched themselves to the flag_ (lines 24–25) means

   a. most people did sewing for their first job.
   b. people began to adapt to the new country.

5. According to the last paragraph, the owner

   a. was happy that Mameh was working faster and getting more sewing done.
   b. gave Mameh money for the rent.

D. **DISCUSSION.** America has been called "the land of freedom and opportunity." Do you think that this is true? Use information from the reading to support your opinion.

THE HISTORY OF POLLUTION

A. **PREDICTING.** Read the first two lines of this article.

1. What do you think will follow?

   a. A serious, factual description of the history of pollution.
   b. A light, humorous essay on pollution.

Washington.—Everyone talks about water pollution, but no one seems to know who started it. The history of modern water pollution in the United States goes back to February 28, 1931, when Mrs. Frieda Murphy leaned over her back-yard fence and said to Mrs. Sophie Holbrook, "You call those shirts white?" Mrs. Holbrook blushed and said, "They're as white as I can get them with this ordinary laundry soap."

— "What you should use is this *Formula Cake Soap* which guarantees against the dull wash-tub grey look that the family wash always had."

Skeptical but adventurous, Mrs. Holbrook tried the *Formula* soap, which happily did take the grey out of her husband's shirts. But what Mrs. Holbrook didn't know was that after the water was  drained from the tub, it emptied into the sewer, which emptied into the Blue Sky River, killing two fish.

Three years later, Mrs. Murphy leaned over the fence and said to Mrs. Holbrook, "It's none of my business, but are you still using that *Formula Cake Soap?*"

— "Yes, I am."

— "No wonder your husband's shirts always look dirty around the collar."

— "I can never get the dirt off the collar," Mrs. Holbrook cried.

— "You can, if you use *Klonk Soap Chips*. They were designed especially for collar dirt. Here, you can have my box."

Mrs. Holbrook used the *Klonk* and the next time her husband put on his shirt he remarked, "How on earth did you get the collar clean?"

— "That's my secret," said Mrs. Holbrook, and then she whispered to no one in particular, "and Mrs. Murphy's."

But unbeknownst to Mrs. Holbrook, the water from *Klonk Soap Chips* prevented any fish downstream from hatching eggs. Four years later, Mrs. Murphy was hanging up her shirts and Mrs. Holbrook said, "How did you ever get your cuffs so white, surely not with *Klonk*?"

— "Not ordinary *Klonk*," Mrs. Murphy said. "But I did with *Super Fortified Klonk* with the XLP additive. You see, *Super Fortified Klonk* attacks dirt and destroys it. Here, try some on your shirts."

Mrs. Holbrook did and discovered her husband's shirt cuffs turned pure white. What she could not possibly know was that it turned the river water pure white as well. The years went by, and poor Mrs. Murphy died. Her daughter-in-law took over the house. Mrs. Holbrook noticed how the daughter-in-law used to sing as she hung up her wash. "Why do you always sing?" asked Mrs. Holbrook.

— "Because of this *Dynamite* detergent. It literally dynamites my clothes clean. Here, try it, and then let's go to a movie, since *Dynamite* detergent takes the drudgery out of washing."

Six months later the Blue Sky River was declared a health hazard.

Finally last year Mrs. Murphy's daughter-in-law called over to Mrs. Holbrook, "Have you heard about *Zap,* the enzyme giant killer?"

A few days later, as Mr. Holbrook was walking home from work, he accidentally fell into the Blue Sky River, swallowed a mouthful of water and died immediately.

At the funeral service the minister said, "You can say anything you want about Holbrook, but no one can deny he had the cleanest shirts in town."

Art Buchwald
in the *International Herald Tribune*

B. DISCUSSING YOUR PREDICTION. Was the prediction you made after reading the first two lines of the article correct? Why do you think that the author begins with a serious tone and then shifts unexpectedly to humorous anecdotes? What other lines from the article are unexpected and therefore funny?

What is it? What looks like winter ice clogging a river is actually acres of foam created by detergents which contribute greatly to water pollution.

C. INTERPRETING LANGUAGE. Circle the correct answer.

1. When Mrs. Murphy says, "You call those shirts white?", she is

   a. asking for information.
   b. criticizing her neighbor.

2. When Mrs. Murphy says, "What you should use is this *Formula Cake Soap* which guarantees against the dull wash-tub grey look that the family wash always had," she sounds like

   a. a close friend giving advice.
   b. a person on a TV commercial.

3. According to the article, Mrs. Holbrook wants to have whiter clothes

   a. to please her husband.
   b. so she doesn't have to buy new clothes.

D. DISCUSSION

1. The first detergent is described as guaranteeing "against the dull wash-tub grey look that the family wash always had." Each new detergent sounds more powerful than the last. What are the words or phrases that are used to give this idea? Do you think they are effective? Why or why not?

   _____

   _____

   _____

   _____

2. In what way does "The History of Pollution" justify the Indians' criticisms of the white man?

Daddy, what did you do in the war against pollution?

Of course you can always try to change the subject.

But one answer you can't give is that you weren't in it. Because in this war, there are no 4 F's and no conscientious objectors. No deferments for married men or teen-agers. And no exemptions for women.

So like it or not, we're all in this one. But as the war heats up, millions of us stay coolly uninvolved. We have lots of alibis:

What can one person do?

It's up to "them" to do something about pollution — not me.

Besides, average people don't pollute. It's the corporations, institutions and municipalities.

The fact is that companies and governments are made up of people. It's people who make decisions and do things that foul up our water, land and air. And that goes for businessmen, government officials, housewives or homeowners.

What can one person do for the cause? Lots of things — maybe more than you think. Like cleaning your spark plugs every 1000 miles, using detergents in the recommended amounts, by upgrading incinerators to reduce smoke emissions, by proposing and supporting better waste treatment plants in your town. Yes, and throwing litter in a basket instead of in the street.

Above all, let's stop shifting the blame. People start pollution. People can stop it. When enough Americans realize this we'll have a fighting chance in the war against pollution.

Keep America Beautiful

People start pollution. People can stop it.

A. UNDERSTANDING VOCABULARY IN CONTEXT. Circle the correct answer.

1. *4 F's* and *conscientious objectors* (paragraph 2)

   a. went to war.
   b. didn't go to war.

2. *Alibis* (paragraph 3) are

   a. excuses for not doing something.
   b. complaints.

3. *Municipalities* (paragraph 6) are

   a. cities.
   b. factories.

4. *Foul up* (paragraph 7) means

   a. make better.
   b. make worse.

5. *Upgrading* (paragraph 8) means

   a. making better.
   b. making worse.

6. *Shifting the blame* (last paragraph) means

   a. saying that you're doing something wrong.
   b. saying that someone else is doing something wrong.

B. DEBATE

Pollution is inevitable because people are not ready to change their habits.

Garden City

Garden City is a real city in Kansas.

Anyone who has made the coast-to-coast journey across America, whether by train or by car, has probably passed through Garden City, but it is reasonable to assume that few travelers remember the event. It seems just another fair-sized town in the middle — almost the exact middle — of the continental United States. Not that the inhabitants would tolerate such an opinion — perhaps rightly. Though they may overstate the case ("Look all over the world, and you won't find friendlier people or fresher air or sweeter drinking water", and "I could go to Denver at triple the salary, but I've got five kids, and I figure there's no better place to raise kids than right here. Swell schools with every kind of sport. We even have a junior college", and "I came out here to practice law. A temporary thing; I never planned to stay. But when the chance came to move, I thought, Why go ? What the hell for ? Maybe it's not New York — but who wants New York ? Good neighbors, people who care about each other, that's what counts. And everything else a decent man needs — we've got that too. Beautiful churches. A golf course'.'), the newcomer to Garden City, once he has adjusted to the nightly after-eight silence of Main Street, discovers much to support the defensive boastings of the citizenry : a well-run public library, a competent daily newspaper, green-lawned and shady squares here and there, placid residential streets where animals and children are safe to run free, a big, rambling park, complete with a small menagerie ("See the Polar Bears !" "See Penny the Elephant !"), and a swimming pool that consumes several acres ("World's Largest FREE Swim-Pool !"). Such accessories, and the dust and the winds and the ever-calling train whistles add up to a "home town" that is probably remembered with nostalgia by those who have left it, and that, for those who have remained, provides a sense of roots and contentment.

Without exception, Garden Citians deny that the population of the town can be socially graded ("No, sir, nothing like that here. All equal regardless of wealth, color, or creed. Everything the way it ought to be in a democracy; that's us"), but of course, class distinctions are as clearly observed, and as clearly observable, as in any other human hive. A hundred miles west and one would be out of the "Bible Belt", that Gospel-haunted strip of American territory in which a man must, if only for business reasons, take his religion with the straightest of faces, but in Finney County one is still within the Bible Belt borders, and therefore a person's church affiliation is the most important factor influencing his class status. A combination of Baptists, Methodists, and Roman Catholics would account for eighty per cent of the county's devout, yet among the elite — the businessmen, bankers, lawyers, physicians, and more prominent ranchers who tenant the top drawer — Presbyterians and Episcopalians dominate. An occasional Methodist is welcomed, and once in a while a Democrat infiltrates, but on the whole the Establishment is composed of right-wing Republicans of the Presbyterian and Episcopalian faiths.

Truman Capote : *In Cold Blood*

10

15

20

25

30

35

A. UNDERSTANDING CONTEXTUAL REFERENCE. Fill in the blanks.

1. *The event* (line 3) refers to _____.

2. A *temporary thing* (line 10) refers to _____.

3. *That* (line 14) refers to _____.

4. *Such accessories* (line 21) refers to _____

   _____.

5. *Those who have remained* (lines 23–24) refers to _____

   _____.

6. *All* (line 26) refers to _____.

7. *The elite* (line 35) refers to _____

   _____.

B. UNDERSTANDING VOCABULARY IN CONTEXT. Circle the correct answer.

1. A *fair-sized town* (line 3) is probably

    a. a very small town.
    b. not a very small town.

2. To *overstate the case* (line 6) probably means

    a. to exaggerate.
    b. to get angry.

3. *Placid . . . streets* (line 18) are probably

    a. quiet and peaceful.
    b. noisy and busy.

4. *Without exception* (line 25) means

    a. everyone.
    b. almost everyone.

5. A *creed* (line 27) is probably

    a. a religious affiliation.
    b. a job.

6. The *Bible Belt* (line 29) is

    a. a type of church.
    b. a geographic area where religion is very important.

C. COMPOSITION. You are spending a month in Garden City as an exchange student. Write a letter to a friend giving your frank impressions of the place and of the people.

D. DEBATE

It is more pleasant to live in a place like Garden City than in a big city.

"A lot of people [...] hate the country and love congestion. It's all very well to say, "Who wants to live in Brooklyn?" — but the answer is, three million people do, and just try to move any of them."

Robert Moses*

What Men? What Needs?

Many beautiful areas in many parts of the Southwest are far less accessible and far less frequented than Grand Canyon. Some of them I have visited again and again during the course of twenty years but never without seeing some evidence of human activity which had diminished or destroyed things I had come to enjoy. Something precious had disappeared because it could not coexist with energetic exploitation. 5

"Oh, well," I have sometimes said to myself, "most of it will probably outlast my time." But I have never been completely comforted by the thought. All concern for posterity aside, I do not like to think that something I have loved may cease to be, even when I am no longer here to take my joy of it.

Perhaps no radical and permanent solution of the problem is possible. The world 10
grows more crowded year by year and at an ever increasing rate. Men push farther and farther in their search for "resources" to be exploited, even for more mere space to occupy. Increasingly they tend to think of the terrestrial globe as *their* earth. They never doubt their right to deal with it as they think fit — and what they think fit usually involves the destruction of what nature has thought fit during many 15
millions of years.

Only the United States among highly developed nations can still offer its citizens the opportunity to visit large regions where nature still dominates the scene. And that is because only the United States began at a sufficiently early stage of its development to set aside as public lands some of the most attractive of such regions. 20

We had national parks before England had established so much as one small nature reserve. In so far as this is true it suggests hope. We have not been entirely blind to what we have, nor to the danger of losing it. [...]

How much longer the check will hold is uncertain; and there are signs that the American people — or at least its leaders — are less concerned than was the generation of Theodore Roosevelt to preserve for posterity some of the wild portions of our heritage. 25

No one opposes "conservation" as such. But many insist upon defining it in their own way. [...]

Those who would cut the timber, slaughter the animals as game, turn cattle loose 30 to graze, flood the area with dams, or even open them up to real estate subdivision are fond of saying, "After all, human needs come first". But of what needs and of what human beings are we thinking? Of the material needs (or rather profits) of a few ranchers and lumbermen, or of the mental and physical health, the education and spiritual experiences, of a whole population? We do not tear down a high school 35 because the building industry can prove that it could profitably erect an apartment house on the site and that tenants would be glad to occupy it. We say, instead, that education pays off in a different way and that the space occupied by schools is not wasted. Much the same thing we say also of the space taken up by the green of a city square. But if parks and other public lands are to be held only until someone can 40 show that a "use" has been found for them, they will not last very much longer. If we recognize that there is more than one kind of utility and that the parks are, at the present moment, being put to the best use to be found for them, then they may last a long time — until, perhaps, overpopulation has reached the point where the struggle for mere animal survival is so brutal that no school or theater, no concert hall or 45 church, can be permitted to "waste" the land on which it stands.

Joseph Wood Krutch: *Grand Canyon*

---

* *Robert Moses* : For 40 years head of both the New York and Long Island State Park Commissions and as such creator of numerous public equipment in or immediately outside New York City.

A. LOCATING SPECIFIC INFORMATION. Fill in the correct information.

1. Why does the author feel sad about the destruction of natural beauty? _____

    _____

2. In paragraph 3 the author gives two reasons why *no radical and permanent solution . . . is possible*. What are they? _____

    _____

3. What is the evidence that the author cites in paragraph 4 to show that *we have not been entirely blind to what we have, nor to the danger of losing it*? _____

    _____

4. What are the signs that protecting natural reserves is less important to some people now? (paragraph 7) _____

    _____

5. Why may the parks and public lands be destroyed some day? (paragraph 7) _____

    _____

B. DISCUSSION. *We say . . . that education pays off . . . and that the space occupied by schools is not wasted. Much the same thing we say also of the space taken up by the green of a city square.* Do you agree with the author's comparison? Why or why not?

Fuel for the future– will America have enough?

Tell Congress what you think it should do to conserve and develop energy.

The page opposite belongs to you. Use it to spur Congress to enact a much-needed energy policy for our nation.

Tell your Congressman — in your own words and for your own reasons — what you think America must do to develop the energy we need for the future. Energy to keep our lights burning. Our homes heated. Our automobiles running. Our factories working.

Conservation can help

All of us must seek new and better ways to save energy — right now and for years to come. But conservation is no cure-all. If America is to grow, and to become less dependent on foreign fuel, reliable sources of domestic energy must be developed.

Coal and nuclear power are practical answers

America sits squarely on top of one of the largest supplies of coal on earth — enough to last hundreds of years, even if we double or triple present levels of consumption.

As a nation, we should expand coal production and substitute this fuel for dwindling supplies of gas and oil.

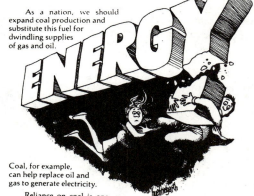

Coal, for example, can help replace oil and gas to generate electricity.

Reliance on coal is one answer. Increasing the share of the nation's electric power that comes from nuclear energy is another answer. Without continued expansion of safe, large-scale nuclear power, there's a good chance America will face energy shortages year after year as demand rises.

Tell Washington to act
Your ideas on energy may differ from ours. What matters is that you let Washington know what you think. And that you want action.

Write your Congressman today. Your message — along with the messages of thousands of other voters — won't go unheeded.

Bethlehem

Bethlehem Steel Corporation
Bethlehem, PA 18016

A. UNDERSTANDING THE AUTHOR'S PURPOSE. Circle the correct answers. Then discuss them.

1. ''Fuel for the future—will America have enough?'' is

   a. a newspaper article on energy.
   b. an advertisement paid for by Bethlehem Steel.
   c. an advertisement paid for by Congress.

2. Which of these points would the authors of this article want the reader to bring up in a letter to Congress?

   a. Changing our habits to conserve more energy is the only way to solve our fuel problems.
   b. We must improve our relations with foreign oil exporting countries so they can supply us with the fuel we need.
   c. We should expand coal production.
   d. We should invest more money in discovering and developing new sources of gas and oil.
   e. We should expand the production of nuclear energy.

B. DISCUSSION. *Your ideas on energy may differ from ours. What matters is that you let Washington know what you think.* Do you think the authors mean this? Why or why not?

C. DEBATE

1. Pollution is the price we must pay for progress.

2. Nuclear energy is the energy of the future.

By permission of Johnny Hart and Field Enterprises, Inc.

IV. The American Mosaic

THE REAL AMERICA ?

In 1975, Mr Egon Bahr, West Germany's Minister for Economic Development and previously Minister for Foreign Affairs, decided to turn his vacation into an unofficial adventure and to try to discover the real America, beyond the hotel and conference rooms of Washington, D.C., and New York City. Flying to San Francisco, Mr Bahr and his wife Dorothea rented a car and for 30 days toured across the U.S.. Later on he summed up his reaction for a Time journalist in a candid interview.

On the scale of the U.S.

It was fascinating to see that this gigantic land has created an average level of civilization that covers the entire country. This is a fantastic achievement that Americans are not even aware
5   of. Everyone in America is an American. That is one of my strongest impressions. It is almost unimportant whether their ancestors came from Ireland, Italy, Greece, Germany. The uniting bond is much stronger than such differences.
10 The differences between East and West are also much less than I had thought. All my friends told me to fly from Denver to Chicago because it is a long distance with nothing to see. That is not true at all. There is a great deal to see. Only
15 after seeing it is it possible to know how much corn and wheat there is. You have to measure out the distance and size up yourself to get a conception of the vastness of the country.

On U.S. isolation

For two weeks I was not able to get an idea of
20 what was going on in the world from the newspapers, radio and television stations I encountered on the way. I was, just like most Americans, on an island — to my dismay. The people are terribly ignorant. I talked to some
25 people from Rapid City, S. Dak., who asked me in all seriousness how we "got around" in Germany. I did not understand the question and asked what they meant, and they then asked, did we get around in Germany on bicycles ?
30 That amazed me. There is something admirable about the way they live their lives and do not know what is happening in the world. But it is also alarming, alarming in the highest degree, that the mass of the population has no idea of
35 the responsibility that their country has in the world. I hope that the leaders in Washington will always be strong enough to act on their understanding of U.S. responsibilities in the face of the lethargy of the majority. I must count
40 on the people who have the responsibility to live up to it, although they know it is not easy.

On U.S. television

When I came back, I was almost without criticism for West German television because in America I felt that the media are in the process
45 of making themselves superfluous. There are so many advertisements they kill one another off. We were sometimes disgusted that on television one series would follow another with the violence getting stronger each time. One gets the impression that only violence is acceptable   50
as entertainment.

On the U.S. diet

I liked the steaks, the Italian food and corn on the cob. Otherwise, I think it is frightful to have to live on hamburgers, especially when the alternative seems to be hot dogs. I found the   55
food unimaginative, boring, with the exception of steaks, but I cannot eat steaks every day. First I thought that the beer was too weak to run out of the bottle, but after a while, it began to taste good, probably because the weather was   60
very, very warm.

On Americans

I got the impression from many people that they felt condescending toward Europeans and were thinking : "You poor creatures, you come from Germany, from Europe. It is very far,   65
probably cold, and you are certainly poor. Here is the most beautiful, the best, the biggest, the most progressive, the most wonderful country in the world." That is the generally uncritical attitude I detected.   70

On minorities

I made a few excursions to Indian reservations and had the feeling that on this point America reveals its bad conscience. I would find the Bicentennial an excellent opportunity to correct something here. As for black-white   75
relations, I have found over the years in both New York and Washington relaxed situations and occasions when I saw naked hatred in the eyes of a black person. This time I found a relaxed situation — to my surprise.   80

On crime and violence

One of the most positive points of all is in a way the opposite of violence. I drove more than 5,000 miles and never saw an auto accident. This would not be possible in Germany; in fact it would not be possible anywhere in Europe. I   85
did not see any crime on our travels, although everyone warned us to lock up the car and not to leave anything in it. I never felt danger.

On returning to the U.S.

The country is made for traveling, and for traveling by car. The certain result of this trip is   90
my appetite to see the South and the North.

From *Time* September 22, 1975

A. UNDERSTANDING CONTEXTUAL REFERENCE. Fill in the blanks.

1. *This* (line 3) refers to _____.

2. *Such differences* (line 9) refers to _____.

3. *That* (line 13) refers to _____.

4. *Here* (line 66) refers to _____.

5. *This point* (line 72) refers to _____.

6. *Here* (line 75) refers to _____.

B. UNDERSTANDING VOCABULARY IN CONTEXT/DISCUSSION. You might
not understand the meaning of some of the words or expressions that you just read.
Work in groups and try to figure out the meaning of these words using other information
from the reading or your own experience.

scale (first subtitle)
vastness (line 18)
alarming (line 33)
lethargy (line 39)
count on (lines 39–40)
disgusted (line 47)
condescending (line 63)

C. INFERRING MEANING. Write *T* for true or *F* for false.

_____ 1. Before starting on his trip, Mr. Bahr thought that the East was very different from the West.

_____ 2. Between Denver and Chicago, the Bahrs saw a lot of farmland.

_____ 3. Mr. Bahr thinks the Americans don't know what's going on in the world because they don't read the newspapers.

_____ 4. Mr. Bahr feels that leaders in Washington are also ignorant of U.S. responsibilities in the world.

_____ 5. Mr. Bahr was upset by the violence in many of the television advertisements.

_____ 6. He was afraid to eat the hamburgers because he thought they might make him sick.

_____ 7. Mr. Bahr was very impressed by the favorable conditions on the Indian reservations.

D. DISCUSSION. *Everyone in America is an American.* What does Mr. Bahr mean by this statement?

Nikki Rosa

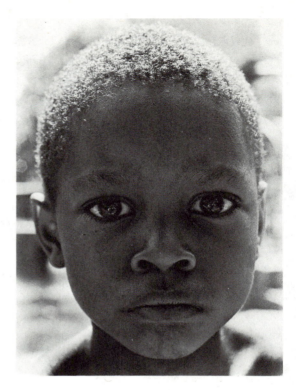

childhood remembrances are always a drag
if you're Black
you always remember things like living in Woodlawn[1]
with no inside toilet
and if you become famous or something
they never talk about how happy you were to have your mother
all to yourself and
how good the water felt when you got your bath from one of those
big tubs that folks in Chicago barbecue in
and somehow when you talk about home
it never gets across how much you
understood their feelings
as the whole family attended meetings about Hollydale[1]
and even though you remember
your biographers never understand
your father's pain as he sells his stock
and another dream goes
and though you're poor it isn't poverty that
concerns you
and though they fought a lot
it isn't your father's drinking that makes any difference
but only that everybody is together and you
and your sister have happy birthdays and very good Christmases
and I really hope no white person ever has cause to write about me
because they never understand Black love is Black wealth and they'll
probably talk about my hard childhood and never understand that
all the while I was quite happy

Nikki Giovanni : Black Judgement

---

1. Woodlawn, Hollydale: parts of the Chicago ghetto.

A. UNDERSTANDING VOCABULARY IN CONTEXT. Circle the correct answer.

1. A *drag* is probably something

   a. pleasant.
   b. unpleasant.

2. *Woodlawn* is probably a _____ neighborhood.

   a. poor
   b. middle class

3. To *barbecue* probably means

   a. to take a bath.
   b. to cook.

4. *Stock* is probably

   a. animals.
   b. investments.

B. COMPOSITION/DISCUSSION. Why does the poet object to the way white people generally visualize a black childhood? Write a composition or discuss your ideas.

ON THE ROAD

A. PREDICTING. Read the first paragraph. Then circle the correct answer.

1. What do you think the author will describe in the next paragraphs?

   a. The interesting places he saw on his trip.
   b. The people he met on the truck.

The greatest ride in my life was about to come up, a truck, with a flatboard at the back, with about six or seven boys sprawled out on it, and the drivers, two young blond farmers from Minnesota, were picking up every single soul they found on that road — the most smiling, cheerful couple of handsome bumpkins you could ever wish to see, both wearing cotton shirts and overalls, nothing else; both thick-wristed   5
and earnest, with broad howareyou smiles for anybody and anything that came across their path. I ran up, said "Is there room?" They said, "Sure, hop on, 'sroom for everybody."

I wasn't on the flatboard before the truck roared off; I lurched, a rider grabbed me, and I sat down. Somebody passed a bottle of rotgut, the bottom of it. I took a   10
big swig in the wild, lyrical, drizzling air of Nebraska. "Whooee, here we go!" yelled a kid in a baseball cap, and they gunned up the truck to seventy and passed

everybody on the road. "We been riding this sonofabitch since Des Moines. These guys never stop. Every now and then you have to yell for pisscall, otherwise you have to piss off in the air, and hang on, brother, hang on."   15

I looked at the company. There were two young farmer boys from North Dakota in red baseball caps, which is the standard North Dakota farmer-boy hat, and they were headed for the harvests; their old men had given them leave to hit the road for a summer. There were two young city boys from Columbus, Ohio, high-school football players, chewing gum, winking, singing in the breeze, and said they were   20 hitchhiking around the United States for the summer. "We're going to L.A. !" they yelled.

— "What are you going to do there ?"

— "Hell, we don't know. Who cares ?"

Then there was a tall slim fellow who had a sneaky look. "Where you from ?" I   25 asked. I was lying next to him on the platform; you couldn't sit without bouncing off, it had no rails. And he turned slowly to me, opened his mouth, and said, "Montana".

Finally there were Mississippi Gene and his charge. Mississippi Gene was a little dark guy who rode freight trains around the country, a thirty-year-old hobo but with   30 a youthful look so you couldn't tell exactly what age he was. And he sat on the boards crosslegged, looking out over the fields without saying anything for hundreds of miles, and finally at one point he turned to me and said, "Where *you* headed ?"...

I said Denver.

— "I got a sister there but I ain't seed her for several couple years." His language   35 was melodious and slow. He was patient. His charge was a sixteen-year-old tall blond kid, also in hobo rags; that is to say, they wore old clothes that had been turned black by the soot of railroads and the dirt of boxcars and sleeping on the ground. The blond kid was also quiet and he seemed to be running away from something, and it figured to be the law the way he looked straight ahead and wet his   40 lips in worried thought. Montana Slim spoke to them occasionally with a sardonic and insinuating smile. They paid no attention to him. Slim was all insinuation. I was afraid of his long goofy grin that he opened up straight in your face and held there half-moronically.

— "You got any money ?" he said to me.   45

— "Hell, no, maybe enough for a pint of whisky till I get to Denver. What about you ?"

— "I know where I can get some."

— "Where ?"

— "Anywhere. You can always folly a man down an alley, can't you ?"   50

— "Yeah, I guess you can."

— "I ain't beyond doing it when I really need some dough. Headed up to Montana to see my father. I'll have to get off this rig at Cheyenne and move up some other way. These crazy boys are going to Los Angeles."

— "Straight ?"   55

— "All the way — if you want to go to L.A. you got a ride."

I mulled this over; the thought of zooming all night across Nebraska, Wyoming, and the Utah desert in the morning, and then most likely the Nevada desert in the afternoon, and actually arriving in Los Angeles within a foreseeable space of time almost made me change my plans. But I had to go to Denver. I'd have to get off at   60 Cheyenne too, and hitch south ninety miles to Denver.

I was glad when the two Minnesota farmboys who owned the truck decided to stop in North Platte and eat; I wanted to have a look at them. They came out of the cab and smiled at all of us. "Pisscall !" said one. "Time to eat !" said the other. But they were the only ones in the party who had money to buy food. We all shambled   65 after them to a restaurant run by a bunch of women, and sat around over hamburgers and coffee while they wrapped away enormous meals just as if they were back in their mother's kitchen. They were brothers; they were transporting farm machinery from Los Angeles to Minnesota and making good money at it. So on their trip to the Coast empty they picked up everybody on the road. They'd done 70 this about five times now; they were having a hell of a time. They liked everything. They never stopped smiling. I tried to talk to them — a kind of dumb attempt on my part to befriend the captains of our ship — and the only responses I got were two sunny smiles and large white corn-fed teeth.

Jack Kerouac : On the Road

B. DISCUSSING YOUR PREDICTION. Now that you've finished reading, was your prediction right? What clues can you find in the first paragraph that suggest that Kerouac will be talking about people more than places?

C. UNDERSTANDING VOCABULARY IN CONTEXT. Fill in the blanks.

1. Two words (line 2) that mean "lying down": _____ .
2. A word (line 4) that refers to the Minnesota farmers: _____ .
3. A word (line 10) that means "cheap liquor": _____ .
4. A word (line 11) that shows it was raining a little: _____ .
5. Two words (line 18) that mean "father": _____ .
6. Two words (lines 26–27) that mean "falling off": _____ .
7. A word (line 30) used to describe a man who rides freight trains: _____ .
8. A phrase (line 33) that means "Where are you going?": _____

   _____ .

9. Two words (line 37) used to describe the old clothes the blond kid was wearing:

   _____ .

10. A word (line 44) that means "stupidly": _____ .
11. Slang for "rob" (line 50): _____ .
12. Slang for "money" (line 52): _____ .
13. A phrase (line 57) that means "thought about something": _____

    _____ .

14. A phrase (line 71) that means "having a good time": _____

    _____ .

D. DISCUSSION. What different aspects of America did the different boys on the platform represent?

American cowboys today.

SAN ANTONIO, TEX.
Where the Cowboy Was Born

A. PREDICTING

1. Discuss the title of this article. What do you already know about San Antonio? Texas? Cowboys? What cowboy (Western) movies have you seen? How did cowboys dress? What did they do? What was the "Old West" like?

2. Discuss the meaning of these words before you read the article.
   trail drives
   rodeo
   country and western music

Though the trail drives have gone the way of the Old West, you still find cowboys here, city cowboys like Edd Owen, who rents a run-down, one-horse spread on the outskirts of San Antonio, about a 20-minute drive from downtown. He ekes out a living in today's world as a concrete form settler, but just looking at him — 7 feet from boots to hat — and listening to him talk, no one would mistake Edd for anything but a cowboy.

"Just a Texan," he corrected me, "actin' kind of natural."

Edd is a rodeo buff, he listens to country and western music, he loves his beer and tequila, and during the late-fall season, he does little else but hunt the fleet and canny white-tailed deer, probably the most sought-after animal in all Texas.

He and his two boys, Monty and Marlon, don't have to go far to hunt, since deer roam the live oak and mesquite[1] woods on their land. They just have to remember not to shoot in the direction of neighbors or the highway. The day before I stopped by, 9-year-old Marlon had just bagged his first deer, and the head with its eight-point antlers hung from the big pecan tree in their front yard.

"That deer meat comes in handy," Edd said. "We ain't been eatin' too high on the hog lately, work bein' scarce an' all. There's nothin' quite like killin' your first deer; right, Marlon?" Marlon blushed and nodded as his father tousled his hair. "Now he's a deer-slayer. He's come of age."

From *National Geographic Magazine*
April 1976

---

1. mesquite: a spiny tree or shrub of the southwestern states.

B. UNDERSTANDING SYNTAX. Circle the correct answer.

1. *Though the trail drives have gone the way of the Old West* (lines 1–2) means

    a. at present there are trail drives in Texas.
    b. there are no trail drives in Texas now.

2. *No one would mistake Edd for anything but a cowboy* (lines 10–11) means

    a. Edd looks like a cowboy.
    b. Edd does not look like a cowboy.

3. *He does little else but hunt* (lines 16–17) means

    a. he hunts a lot.
    b. he doesn't hunt very much.

C. UNDERSTANDING VOCABULARY IN CONTEXT. Circle the correct answer.

1. *A run-down, one-horse spread* (lines 4–5) is probably

    a. a large ranch that's in very good condition.
    b. a small ranch that's not in very good condition.

2. He *ekes out a living* (lines 6–7) probably means

    a. he makes a lot of money.
    b. he makes very little money.

3. A *sought-after animal* (lines 18–19) is probably

    a. an animal that people like to hunt.
    b. a beautiful animal.

D. DISCUSSION. What do you think of Edd Owen? In what way does he participate in the American Dream?

BIG MONEY, HARD JOB

ANCHORAGE, Alaska (NYT).
— Pat Schnabel is 27, and she's a construction worker. For the past 16 months she has worked in Alaska as a crane operator helping to build the oil pipeline now under construction across the state. During the next year she expects to earn more than $56,000 working 12-hour days and seven-day weeks.

Miss Schnabel looks tough, her brown, shoulder-length hair hangs limply. Her jeans are baggy, her construction boots coated with mud, her blue work-shirt hangs loosely, denying any defined shape beneath it. While Miss Schnabel's appearance seems to lack arrangement, her "look" has been carefully conceived and calculated. "I always wear jeans, three shirts, no make-up," she said. "I de-emphasize my feminity. I have to. The men totally resented me, they totally resent the thought of any woman making as much money as a man."

She admits that the only reason she is out there operating a crane in the mud, in the snow, in the rain, in sub-zero temperatures, is that the money is good. And there is no other job in the world that is going to give her that kind of money.

While no one is keeping track of the figures, oil pipeline officials estimate that women "man" about 10 % of the 20,000 jobs. Most of the women are in traditionally female occupations. They are employed as clerks or secretaries, as kitchen helpers, in the laundries. A smaller percentage work "on the line", driving trucks, operating cranes, working as security guards, drillers or riveters.

Like men on the pipeline, the women are largely motivated by the money. But that's not all. While many men first came to Alaska for the adventure, for money, to get away from bad personal situations back home, women now "escape" to the pipeline for the same reasons.

Most pipeline workers work 82-hour weeks for up to nine straight weeks, then take one or two weeks off. Those who work inside the camps, particularly those in the Arctic north where temperatures may fall to 50 below[1], may not venture out of doors for weeks on end. Construction workers leave their camps each morning with their crew and the group is bused to that day's worksite. After 12 hours, the bus, generally wallpapered with *Playboy* centerfolds, comes rumbling back to take them back to the camps for the evening. Workers do not pay for room or board, nor for their flights back to Anchorage on their time off. So if they're lucky and the Internal Revenue Service doesn't take too much in taxes, they can save a lot while working on the line.

Hilary Hilscher has saved a lot and thanks to the pipeline she is now settled cozily into the homesteader's log cabin she and her boyfriend, a construction foreman, bought in Fairbanks with their "oil money". Miss Hilscher, 27, is typical of many young people on the pipeline. Last fall she left an already well-paying professional job in Juneau where she served as deputy director of telecommunications in the governor's office.

"I saw all my friends making these incredible sums of money, and I guess like the rest of the young people up here, I decided to get it while I could," Miss Hilscher said.

The pipeline life bears "little resemblance to the real world". The hours, the surroundings, the living conditions are no less real than the money. As one woman pointed out, very few women stay "single" in the camps — "living together" is tacitly approved.

Some women link up with a man purely as a means of survival — if they are "taken", the other men won't hassle them as much.

As one woman puts it : "You're living in a space capsule. It's like being on the moon. You don't live in the camps, you just exist. The only thing that gives a sense of normalcy in your life is a relationship."

From *The New York Times*, 1977

---

1. 50 below: in °F = −45°C.

A. **UNDERSTANDING THE MAIN IDEA.** Circle the correct answer.

1. Paragraph 1 gives

   a. a description of Pat Schnabel.
   b. a description of the Alaska pipeline project.
   c. a description of what a crane operator does.

2. The most important information in paragraph 2 is

   a. the description of the clothes Pat wears when she works.
   b. the explanation of why she dresses the way she does.
   c. how she feels about her femininity.

3. The most important information in paragraph 3 is

    a. the weather conditions on the job.
    b. why Pat likes her job.
    c. the salaries of other jobs.

4. Paragraph 4 explains

    a. why women decide to work on the pipeline project.
    b. the kinds of jobs that women have on the project.
    c. why so few women work ''on the line.''

5. Paragraph 5 explains

    a. why women decide to work on the pipeline.
    b. how women's reasons for coming to Alaska are different from men's.
    c. how much money women make on the project.

6. Paragraph 6 describes

    a. work conditions on the project.
    b. the work schedule (number of hours, days off, etc.) on the project.
    c. why it is necessary to work such long hours.

7. The conclusion presented in the last three paragraphs is

    a. if a woman is looking for a relationship with a man, the pipeline camps are a good place to go.
    b. there is a lot of sexual freedom in the camps.
    c. having a relationship helps make life in the camps seem less unreal.

B. COMPOSITION. Mrs. Hilscher is worried about her daughter. She cannot understand why Hilary left a good, steady job to go work on the line. Write the letter that Hilary might write home to explain.

C. DISCUSSION. Would you like to have a job on the pipeline? Why or why not?

Sculpture by Oldenburg.

The American Way of Life

Painting by Norman Rockwell.

LIVING ON CREDIT

A. PRE-READING DISCUSSION. Discuss your answers to these questions before reading the interview.

1. Do you use credit cards? Why or why not?
2. If so, do they make your life easier?
3. Have you ever had any problem with them?

An interview with Patricia Higgins, a young housewife living in New York City. Her husband is in television and they travel extensively.

INTERVIEWER : Why did you start using credit cards in the first place ?

MRS HIGGINS : Well, the first credit card came in the mail, without even being solicited. It was from a bank, a Bank Americard I think, or Master Charge. Later on it turned out to be illegal to send cards like that without the customer asking for them. Anyway, it was a way for the banks to hook people, and we got hooked. 5

INTERVIEWER : What do you mean by "hooked" ?

MRS HIGGINS : You see, after that we got used to using the credit card. It's kind of a fantasy. It's as if you're spending money that's not real. You know, Monopoly money. After a while we realized that you couldn't do enough with one card, so we decided to get a bigger, more international and important credit card. 10

INTERVIEWER : What do you use these cards for ?

MRS HIGGINS : Take vacations for example. I can buy my ticket, pay for the hotel, rent a car and do all my shopping on vacation without having any cash.

INTERVIEWER : It certainly sounds as if life is much easier that way.

MRS HIGGINS : Yes, everything is paid for until the bills come. 15

INTERVIEWER : What happens then ?

MRS HIGGINS : They cancel your credit card if you don't pay the bill. But if you have planned it well, you already have gotten another card from another company, which you get when your credit is still good.

INTERVIEWER : When do things finally catch up with you ? 20

MRS HIGGINS : Eventually you wind up suffering more than enjoying because you have to pay more than you ever imagined you spent. When reality hits you in the face, life becomes very difficult.

INTERVIEWER : Can you imagine living without your credit card ?

MRS HIGGINS : It's very difficult to live without those damn cards. I learned the hard way 25 once after getting in over my head in debt. I forced my husband to stop using the cards by taking scissors and cutting up all our cards into little pieces.

INTERVIEWER : So you were able to stop after that ?

MRS HIGGINS : In a way yes, but not completely. I wound up getting more cards eventually. I find it almost impossible to live without them, but now I try harder not 30 to be ridiculous about fulfilling every fantasy immediately. I try to use more checks because you know if you have money in the bank. But a credit card is like magic. You are billed at the end of the month and even then you don't have to pay. They take it over to the next month and even to the third month and only then will they start to sue. 35

INTERVIEWER : What did you mean about fulfilling every fantasy ?

MRS HIGGINS : Well, say you go into a store to buy a vacuum cleaner and it's something that you need but you know you're going to pay with your credit card. It's possible that you will come out with a color T.V. which you can charge with your card.

INTERVIEWER : At that time you are aware that you don't have the money ? 40

MRS HIGGINS : Yes, you know, but you don't think about it realistically. You figure you're going to get the money somehow. You get caught up in the idea of buy now and pay later. So in the end you wind up spending much more money and buying things you don't really need, and would never have bought if you were paying cash.

INTERVIEWER : Do you think some day credit cards will no longer be available ? 45

MRS HIGGINS : I would like to believe that but I can see how I've gotten hooked on them. The whole consumer society is based on them. Without credit cards there would have to be a complete transformation in people's minds in terms of money and what they need. I don't see that happening in the near future. Like they say, time is money and credit cards give you both for free ! ! !   50

B. UNDERSTANDING VOCABULARY IN CONTEXT. Fill in the blanks.

1. *Without the customer asking for them* (line 4) means the same as _____
   _____ in line 2.

2. *We got used to using the credit card* (line 7) means the same as _____
   _____ in line 5.

3. _____ in line 8 is another name for *money that's not real*.

4. *When . . . things finally catch up with you* (line 20) means about the same as _____
   _____ in line 22.

5. _____ in line 26
   means Mrs. Higgins didn't think she had enough money to pay all the bills.

C. DISCUSSION. *Time is money and credit cards give you both for free!* (lines 49–50)
What do you think Mrs. Higgins means by this conclusion?

King Features Syndicate, Inc.

United Feature Syndicate

W. Rathje, professor of anthropology at the University of Arizona, doing research for his course on "Trash." The theme of the course is, "Tell me what you throw away and I'll tell you who you are." What do you think of this statement?

PLASTIC WORLD

American cities are like badger holes, ringed with trash — all of them — surrounded by miles of wrecked and rusting automobiles, and almost smothered with rubbish. Everything we use comes in boxes, cartons, bins, the so-called packaging we love so much. The mountains of things we throw away are much greater than the things we use. In this, if in no other way, we can see the wild and reckless exuberance of our production, and waste seems to be the index. Driving along I thought how in France or Italy every item of these thrown-out things would have been saved and used for something. This is not said in criticism of one system or other but I do wonder whether there will come a time when we can no longer afford our wastefulness — in the rivers, metal wastes everywhere, and atomic wastes and chemical wastes, buried deep in the earth or sunk in the sea. When an Indian village became too deep in its own filth, the inhabitants moved. And we have no place to which to move.[...]

Not far outside of Bangor[1] I stopped at an auto court and rented a room. It wasn't expensive. The sign said "Greatly Reduced Winter Rates". It was immaculate; everything was done in plastics — the floors, the curtain, table tops of stainless burnless plastic, lamp shades of plastic. Only the bedding and the towels were of a natural material. I went to the small restaurant run in conjunction. It was all plastic too — the table linen, the butter dish. The sugar and crackers were wrapped in cellophane, the jelly in a small plastic coffin sealed with cellophane. It was early evening and I was the only customer. Even the waitress wore a sponge-off apron. She wasn't happy, but then she wasn't unhappy. She wasn't anything.[...]

I went back to my clean little room. I don't ever drink alone. It's not much fun. And I don't think I will until I am an alcoholic. But this night I got a bottle of vodka from my stores and took it to my cell. In the bathroom two water tumblers were sealed in cellophane sacks with the words : "These glasses are sterilized for your protection." Across the toilet-seat a strip of paper bore the message : "This seat has been sterilized with ultra-violet light for your protection." Everyone was protecting me and it was horrible. I tore the glasses from their covers. I violated the toilet-seat with my foot. I poured half a tumbler of vodka and drank it and then another. Then I lay deep in hot water in the tub and I was utterly miserable, and nothing was good anywhere.[...]

I remember an old Arab in North Africa, a man whose hands had never felt water. He gave me mint tea in a glass so coated with use that it was opaque, but he handed me companionship, and the tea was wonderful because of it. And without any protection my teeth didn't fall out, nor did running sores develop. I began to formulate a new law describing the relationship of protection to despondency. A sad soul can kill you quicker, far quicker, than a germ.

John Steinbeck : Travels with Charley

---

1. Bangor: a town in Maine.

A. RECOGNIZING SYNONYMS. In paragraph 1, Steinbeck uses different words to refer to the *things we throw away*. List four of them.

_____   _____

_____   _____

B. UNDERSTANDING THE AUTHOR'S PURPOSE. Circle the correct answer.

1. The main idea of paragraph 1 is

   a. everything is made of plastic nowadays.
   b. Americans are very wasteful.
   c. Europeans are very different from Americans.

2. In paragraph 2 Steinbeck wants the reader

   a. to visualize how pretty and clean the motel looked.
   b. to visualize how sterile and unnatural everything looked.
   c. to sympathize with the waitress.

3. In paragraph 3 Steinbeck wants the reader to feel

    a. his loneliness at that moment.
    b. his unhappiness that everything was so clean and therefore so inhuman.
    c. his fear of becoming an alcoholic.

4. In paragraph 4 Steinbeck wants the reader to realize

    a. how much he enjoyed the companionship of the Arab.
    b. how good the tea tasted.
    c. how dirty the glass looked.

C. DEBATE

There is no way of preventing modern society from becoming a ''plastic world.''

''Furthermore, it can be nailed, bored,
cut, or sawed–just like plastic.''

Drawing by Alan Dunn; ©1940, 1968. The New Yorker Magazine, Inc.

Perpetual Care

Dennis passed through and opening the door marked 'Inquiries' found himself in a raftered banqueting-hall. The 'Hindu Love-Song' was here also, gently discoursed from the dark-oak panelling. A young lady rose from a group of her fellows to welcome him, one of that new race of exquisite, amiable, efficient young ladies whom he had met everywhere in the United States. She wore a white smock 5
and over her sharply supported left breast was embroidered the words, *Mortuary Hostess*.

"Can I help you in any way?"

"I came to arrange about a funeral."

"Is it for yourself?" 10

"Certainly not. Do I look so moribund?"

"Pardon me?"

"Do I look as if I were about to die?"

"Why, no. Only many of our friends like to make Before Need Arrangements. Will you come this way?" 15

She led him through the hall into a soft passage. The *décor* here was Georgian[1]. The 'Hindu Love-Song' came to its end and was succeeded by the voice of a nightingale. In a little chintzy parlour he and his hostess sat down to make their arrangements.

"I must first record the Essential Data." 20

He told her his name and Sir Francis's.

"Now, Mr Barlow, what had you in mind? Embalmment of course, and after that incineration or not, according to taste. Our crematory is on scientific principles, the heat is so intense that all inessentials are volatilized. Some people did not like the

thought that ashes of the casket and clothing were mixed with the Loved One's. 25
Normal disposal is by inhumement, entombment, inurnment, or immurement, but
many people just lately prefer insarcophagusment. That is *very* individual. The
casket is placed inside a sealed sarcophagus, marble or bronze, and rests
permanently above ground in a niche in the mausoleum, with or without a personal
stained-glass window above. That, of course, is for those with whom price is not a 30
primary consideration."

"We want my friend buried."

"This is not your first visit to Whispering Glades?"

"Yes."

"Then let me explain the Dream. The Park is zoned. Each zone has its own name 35
and appropriate Work of Art. Zones of course vary in price and within the zones the
prices vary according to their proximity to the Work of Art. We have single sites as
low as fifty dollars. That is in Pilgrims' Rest, a zone we are just developing behind
the Crematory fuel dump. The most costly are those on Lake Isle. They range
about 1,000 dollars. Then there is Lovers' Nest, zoned about a very, very beautiful 40
marble replica of Rodin's famous statue, the Kiss. We have double plots there at 750
dollars the pair. Was your Loved One married?"

"No."

"What was his business?"

"He was a writer." 45

"Ah, then Poets' Corner would be the place for him. We have many of our
foremost literary names there, either in person or as Before Need Reservations.
You are no doubt acquainted with the works of Amelia Bergson?"

"I know of them."

"We sold Miss Bergson a Before Need Reservation only yesterday, under the 50
statue of the prominent Greek poet Homer. I could put your friend right next to
her. But perhaps you would like to see the zone before deciding."

"I want to see everything."

"There certainly is plenty to see. I'll have one of our guides take you round just as
soon as we have all the Essential Data, Mr Barlow. Was your Loved One of any 55
special religion?"

"An agnostic."

"We have two non-sectarian churches in the Park and a number of non-sectarian
pastors. Jews and Catholics seem to prefer to make their own arrangements."

"I believe Sir Ambrose Abercrombie is planning a special service." 60

"Oh, was your Loved One in films, Mr Barlow? In that case he ought to be in
Shadowland."

"I think he would prefer to be with Homer and Miss Bergson."

"Then the University Church would be most convenient. We like to save the
Waiting Ones a long procession. I presume the Loved One was Caucasian?" 65

"No, why did you think that? He was purely English."

"English are purely Caucasian, Mr Barlow. This is a restricted park. The
Dreamer has made that rule for the sake of the Waiting Ones. In their time of trial
they prefer to be with their own people."

"I think I understand. Well, let me assure you Sir Francis was quite white." 70

As he said this there came vividly into Dennis's mind that image which lurked
there, seldom out of sight for long; the sack of body suspended and the face above it
with eyes red and horribly starting from their sockets, the cheeks mottled in indigo
like the marbled end-papers of a ledger and the tongue swollen and protruding like
an end of black sausage. 75

"Let us now decide on the casket."

They went to the show-rooms where stood coffins of every shape and material :
the nightingale still sang in the cornice.

"The two-piece lid is most popular for gentlemen Loved Ones. Only the upper part is then exposed to view." 80

"Exposed to view?"

"Yes, when the Waiting Ones come to take leave."

"But I say, I don't think that will quite do. I've seen him. He's terribly disfigured, you know."

"If there are any special little difficulties in the case you must mention them to our 85 cosmeticians. You will be seeing one of them before you leave. They have never failed yet."

Evelyn Waugh : *The Loved One*

1. Georgian: eighteenth century architectural style in England.

A. UNDERSTANDING VOCABULARY IN CONTEXT. Circle the correct answer.

1. *Exquisite, amiable* and *efficient* (line 4) are probably

   a. complimentary, positive words.
   b. critical, negative words.

2. *Moribund* (line 11) probably means

   a. sad.
   b. dead.

3. Examples of *inessentials* (line 24) are

   a. casket and clothing.
   b. fingers and toes.

4. *Inhumement, entombment, inurnment, immurement* and *insarcophagusment* (lines 26–27) refer to

   a. the treatment given to the body and where it is finally put.
   b. the different sections of the park.
   c. the different types of funeral services.

5. *Those with whom price is not a primary consideration* (lines 30–31) refers to

   a. rich people.
   b. poor people.

6. *Restricted* (line 67) means

   a. only for English people.
   b. only for white people.

7. *Indigo* (line 73) is probably

   a. a color.
   b. a disease.

8. *Disfigured* (line 83) means

   a. old looking.
   b. ugly looking.

B. UNDERSTANDING CONTEXTUAL REFERENCE. Fill in the blanks.

1. *One* (line 4) refers to _____.

2. *That* (line 27) refers to _____.

3. *The most costly* (line 39) refers to _____.

4. *The pair* (line 42) refers to _____.

5. *Their own people* (line 69) refers to _____.

6. *That image* (line 71) refers to _____
   _____.

7. *The upper part* (lines 79–80) refers to _____.

C. USING EUPHEMISMS. Euphemisms are often used to soften the meaning of a strong or unpleasant word or image. In this reading there are several. Match the euphemism on the left with a word or phrase on the right that means the same.

1. gentlemen *d*

2. the Park ____

3. guide ____

4. the Loved One ____

5. friends ____

6. cosmeticians ____

7. Pilgrim's Rest ____

8. Before Need Arrangements ____

9. the Dreamer ____

10. Essential Data ____

11. Lake Isle ____

12. restricted ____

13. Waiting Ones ____

a. customers

b. prepaid funeral

c. the dead person's name and address

d. men

e. the corpse

f. the family of the dead person

g. the boss

h. the cemetery

i. the cheap section of the cemetery

j. the expensive section of the cemetery

k. salesman

l. segregated

m. embalmers

D. DISCUSSION. How does the author convey that the mortuary and Whispering Glades were ridiculous? What is humorous about the text?

The Praying Businessman

"I'm glad you could come, gentlemen," Curtis O'Keefe informed them, as if this meeting had not been planned weeks ahead. "Perhaps, though, before we begin our business it would benefit all of us if we asked the help of Almighty God."

As he spoke, with the ease of long practice the hotelier slipped agilely to his knees, clasping his hands devoutly in front of him. With an expression bordering on resignation, as if he had been through this experience many times before, Ogden Bailey followed suit and, after a moment's hesitation, the younger man Hall assumed the same position.[...]

"Almighty God," Curtis O'Keefe intoned, his eyes closed and pink-cheeked, leonine face serene, "grant us, if it be thy will, success in what we are about to do. We ask thy blessing and thine active help in acquiring this hotel, named for thine own St Gregory. We plead devoutly that we may add it to those already enlisted — by our own organization — in thy cause and held for thee in trust by thy devoted servant who speaketh." Even when dealing with God, Curtis O'Keefe believed in coming directly to the point.

He continued, his face uplifted, the words rolling onward like a solemn flowing river : "Moreover if this be thy will — and we pray it may — we ask that it be done expeditiously and with economy, such treasure as we thy servants possess, not being depleted unduly, but husbanded to thy further use. We invoke thy blessing also, O God, on those who will negotiate against us, on behalf of this hotel, asking that they shall be governed solely according to thy spirit and that thou shalt cause them to exercise reasonableness and discretion in all they do. Finally, Lord, be with us always, prospering our cause and advancing our works so that we, in turn, may dedicate them to thy greater glory, Amen. Now, gentlemen, how much am I going to have to pay for this hotel?"

O'Keefe had already bounced back into his chair. It was a second or two, however, before the others realized that the last sentence was not a part of the prayer, but the opening of their business session. Bailey was first to recover and, springing back adroitly from his knees to the settee, brought out the contents of his briefcase. Hall, with a startled look, scrambled to join him.

Arthur Hailey : *Hotel*

DEAR GOD, - MY
FATHAR SAID KIDS IS
THE BEST TIME IN
LIFE. PLEASE TELL
HIM WHAT GOOD IS IT
IF WE NEVER GET TO STAY
UP AND WATCH ANYTHING.
JO

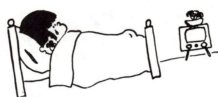

Dear God,
Are boys better
than girls, I
Know you are one
but try to be
fair.

Sylvia.

A. UNDERSTANDING STYLES OF SPEECH.

Formal language is common in prayers because it shows respect. Write the meaning of these words or phrases from the prayer.

1. *. . . grant us . . . success in what we are about to do.* _____

_____

2. *. . . in acquiring this hotel . . .* _____

3. *. . . named for thine own St. Gregory.* _____

4. *We plead devoutly . . .* _____

5. *Moreover, if this be thy will . . .* _____

_____

6. *. . . we ask that it be done expeditiously and with economy . . .* _____

_____

7. *We invoke thy blessing . . .* _____

8. *. . . thou shalt cause them to exercise reasonableness . . .* _____

_____

B. UNDERSTANDING SYNTAX.

Circle the correct answer.

1. *As if this meeting had not been planned weeks ahead* (paragraph 1) means

  a. the meeting had been planned.
  b. the meeting had not been planned.

2. *Before we begin our business it would benefit all of us if we asked the help of Almighty God* (paragraph 1) means

  a. first we have our meeting, and then we pray.
  b. first we pray, and then we have our meeting.

3. *As he spoke . . . the hotelier slipped agilely to his knees* (paragraph 2) means

  a. first he spoke, and then he got to his knees.
  b. he spoke and got to his knees at the same time.

4. *As if he had been through this experience many times before* (paragraph 2) means

  a. he probably has done this before.
  b. he probably has not done this before.

5. *Bailey . . . , springing back adroitly from his knees to the settee, brought out the contents of his briefcase* (last paragraph) means

  a. first Bailey opened his briefcase, and then he got back on the settee.
  b. first Bailey got back on the settee, and then he opened his briefcase.

C. DEBATE.

Compare the two courses offered on page 96 and debate the following:

Traditional religious teaching reinforces sexual stereotypes.

A Shorter Workweek? No!

Critics of the four-day week—the latest experiment in work schedules—are starting to come forward.

Labor. Joseph Cointin, a regional official of the Machinists Union in St Louis is one of these objectors. In a recent comment, he argues that unions should be working toward a four-day week of 32 hours at 40 hours' pay and "not a backbreaking compression of four days into 40 hours." [...]

"This business of working 10-hour days strikes at the heart of what our unions have accomplished for us over the years, and the shift to four 10-hour days in a workweek that is taking place in many sections of the country can only wreak havoc in the universal 8-hour day that unions so long fought for. [...]

Management, Mr Cointin contended, hopes to "make a higher profit off their labor" by saving the expenses of opening the plant for the fifth day and by "cutting overtime costs to the bone".

Criticism also came from a University of Michigan labor-relations expert, Thomas K. Connellan. He said:

"Too many organizations will seize upon the four-day workweek as the cure for such problems as absenteeism and turnover.

"While it is possible that such a novel work schedule will have a short-term effect—perhaps even for as long as several years—it should be remembered that absenteeism is not the basic problem but rather a symptom."

As Mr Connellan sees it, that problem is "that many people have little or no interest in their jobs" and that most jobs "do not challenge the ability of individuals" holding them.

Evidence was cited from psychological testing that the average person uses only about 10 per cent of his ability. Mr Connellan said that the typical business organization demands only a small part of that productivity. [...]

From *U.S. News and World Report*
May 3, 1971

Business. Virginia O. Hayes, company president, [...] says: "A mandatory 35-hour week would only cripple profitable concerns. Fixed employee costs—insurance, disability payments, taxes—would increase because more employees would be needed to produce the same amount of goods. Probably, increased prices would begin to reduce the demand for goods, and the vicious recession cycle would start all over again." [...]

"Cutting the workweek," says William Cosulas, president of a Beverage Company, [...], "would encourage workers to seek additional part-time work for added income and could well keep some of the unemployed from getting jobs." [...]

Robert E. Adams, general manager of an Oil Company, [...] is also against shortening the workweek. "With the already existing coffee breaks, extra holidays on long weekends, sick leave, extended vacations, and many other fringe benefits, it appears to me that we are lucky to get 35 hours of production now," he says.

Thomas R. Henderson company president, [...] feels that "we have enough leisure time now. Quality of life can deteriorate with too little gainful work and too much leisure time."

From *Nation's Business*
March 1976

Each clock = 12 hours
Each dollar bill = $50

WORK HOURS
60 hours per week

LEISURE TIME
24 hours per week

less than $10

RECREATION SPENDING PER PERSON PER YEAR

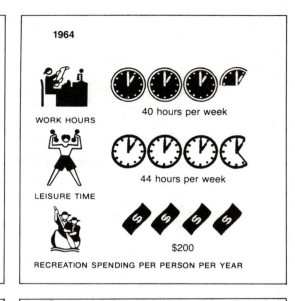

1964

WORK HOURS
40 hours per week

LEISURE TIME
44 hours per week

$200

RECREATION SPENDING PER PERSON PER YEAR

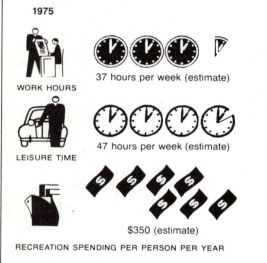

1975

WORK HOURS
37 hours per week (estimate)

LEISURE TIME
47 hours per week (estimate)

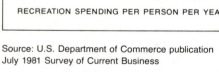

$350 (estimate)

RECREATION SPENDING PER PERSON PER YEAR

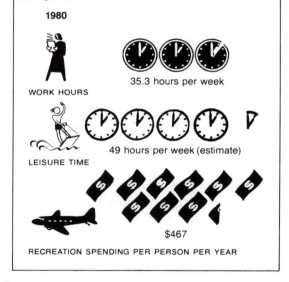

1980

WORK HOURS
35.3 hours per week

LEISURE TIME
49 hours per week (estimate)

$467

RECREATION SPENDING PER PERSON PER YEAR

Source: U.S. Department of Commerce publication
July 1981 Survey of Current Business

$106,414 million dollars per year in recreation spending
227.7 million persons

A. UNDERSTANDING VOCABULARY IN CONTEXT. Circle the correct answer.

1. *Strikes at the heart* (paragraph 2) means

  a. hurts.
  b. destroys.

2. *Shift* (paragraph 2) means

  a. the change.
  b. the work day.

3. *Wreak havoc* (paragraph 2) means

    a. cause some problems.
    b. cause critical problems.

4. *"Cutting overtime costs to the bone"* (paragraph 3) means

    a. reducing costs a little.
    b. reducing costs a lot.

5. *Cripple* (paragraph 9) means

    a. hurt a little.
    b. hurt a lot.

B. RECOGNIZING POINTS OF VIEW. List the major objections to the shorter workweek voiced by Labor and Business.

1. Joseph Cointin _____

_____

2. Thomas K. Connellan _____

_____

3. Virginia O. Hayes _____

_____

4. William Cosulas _____

_____

5. Robert E. Adams _____

_____

6. Thomas R. Henderson _____

_____

C. DISCUSSION

1. Robert E. Adams calls sick leave a "fringe benefit." In your opinion what are basic worker rights and what are "extras"?

2. Thomas R. Henderson, company president, feels that workers have enough leisure time now. "Quality of life can deteriorate with too little gainful work and too much leisure time." Do you think the workers in his company would agree with him? Do you agree?

SELLING AMERICA

A. PREDICTING. In the article "Selling America" you will read two interviews with advertising men—the first in favor of advertising and the second against. In the first interview these three questions will be asked. How do you think they will be answered? Circle your answer.

1. *What do you think of advertising?*

   a. I think it's important and necessary.
   b. I think it has had a negative influence on the American public.

2. *Does advertising try to manipulate people?*

   a. Yes.
   b. No.

3. *How do you try to reach a potential customer?*

   a. Convince him the product is good.
   b. Appeal to his impulses and fears.

These are some of the questions that will be asked in the second interview. How do you think they will be answered? Circle your answer.

4. *How do you, as an advertising man, see the consumer?*

   a. As an intelligent, well-informed person.
   b. As a "space" to be filled with more and more products.

5. *What exactly do you do in your job?*

   a. Try to convince people your product is better even though they're all alike.
   b. Give people the information about the ways your product is better than others.

6. *Do you like your job?*

   a. I love it.
   b. I hate it.

Now read the interviews and see if you predicted correctly.

PRO

Ross Pelletier is 56 years old. He works for one of the largest advertising agencies in the world. As a child he wanted to be a baggageman on a train. Later, when he began to realize how much money he would earn doing that, he started to think that perhaps he could do a little better...

(adapted)

What do you think of advertising?

Advertising is a very fascinating business to me. We think it's a very important business, sometimes not fully understood. [...] But advertising has been so important in mass consumption. [...] There's no sense producing if people are not going to consume what you produce in masses. You need mass consumption to make use of the goods that are turned out by the dozens in the store, you know.

Does advertising try to manipulate people?

A product must stand up in the consumer's hands. I could, by advertising, maybe induce you to try a product. But you will not make a repurchase if it is not satisfactory. [...] So you cannot put anything over — at least, not more than once. And who wants to stay in business putting something over once?

How do you try to reach a potential customer?

You have to tell a real story. One, is to sell him. But it's to let him know he has a choice. Our economy is an economy of choice. We, in this country, under this wonderful system we have, despite the fact that it has some faults, of course, have a tremendous choice. In worldly goods. And while life is more to it than just worldly goods, still, this man has appetites and needs. And here we have this great choice. [...]

CON

Charlie Landesfahr is 34 years old. He is copy chief at a middle-sized advertising agency. He was graduated from an Ivy League college, and toured Europe as a drummer in a jazz band. On occasion, he writes free-lance articles for national magazines.

(adapted)

How do you, as an advertising man, see the consumer?

The consumer is a great big gaping jaw we're all trying to fill up with whatever we can cram down there, and the great hope is that that jaw will keep getting wider and wider. And the more products there are, the more, you know.

What segment of the population is potentially the most profitable one for advertising?

The population explosion is a grand thing for business, of course. My God, think of all the machines we can sell to more people. A third of the population is going to be under the age of twenty in another year or two, I imagine. They got all the money to spend, that's great. We can sell them records and we can sell them cars and dresses and brassieres at that age, and the whole bit. We can make the whole world like us very fast and make a lot of money on it. We can make it an American middle-class universe.

What exactly do you do in your job?

Sell this product against that product. And what you do is try to find reasons why yours is better. If you can't find those, God help you. It takes time to realize they're identical. We're all conditioned to think this soap is different from that soap, until we go to the factory and see them coming off the same production line. There are times when I still believe they're different. It's a belief we have to hold on to.

Do you like your job?

Do I like my job? No. I deplore it. I hate it. I come home sick at night about it. I'm a pretty unhappy guy some nights. And a pretty mean father. I'm not able to divorce myself at five o'clock from what's happened to me all day long — or what I've been making happen to other people. As a consequence, evenings are not always pleasant.

Studs Terkel: *Division Street*

The airline built for professional travelers.

It takes a level head and a loving heart to be a Delta professional.

You meet all kinds of people with all kinds of travel problems in a Delta ticket office. And you have to know all the answers.

But not just pat answers. You try hard to come up with a lower fare, an easier connection, a faster route, a free stopover, whatever's best for the customer.

You could get by with less. A lot of folks wouldn't know the difference. But when it comes to people, a Delta professional couldn't care more. ▲DELTA
The airline run by professionals

Ticket Sales Agent Sandy Johnakin.   A 15-year Delta professional.

Delta is ready when you are.®

B. UNDERSTANDING VOCABULARY IN CONTEXT. Circle the correct answer.

1. *Turned out* (paragraph 1) means

    a. rejected.
    b. sold.

2. *Stand up* (paragraph 2) means

    a. be of good quality.
    b. look good.

3. *Put . . . over* (paragraph 2) means

    a. produce.
    b. deceive.

4. *Cram down* (paragraph 4) means

    a. put something inside something.
    b. close something.

5. *Hold on to* (paragraph 6) means

    a. keep.
    b. reject.

C. COMPOSITION. Based on what you have read, write what Charlie Landesfahr might answer if he were to debate the following points with Ross Pelletier. Then write a composition expressing either Pelletier's or Landesfahr's point of view.

PELLETIER: You cannot put anything over—at least not more than once.

LANDESFAHR: _____

_____

PELLETIER: You have to tell a real story.

LANDESFAHR: _____

_____

PELLETIER: Our economy is an economy of choice.

LANDESFAHR: _____

_____

D. DISCUSSION. Do you think your country has become an "American middle-class universe"? Why or why not?

Thomas James, an avid outdoorsman and busy foundation administrator, sometimes does not go outdoors for seven or eight days at a stretch.

"We've got it all together here; there's not much reason to go outside, especially in this cold weather," he said. He is one of a group of high-rise Chicagoans who live farther from the ground than anyone else in the world, on the 45th to 92nd floors of the John Hancock[1] Center.

The center, sometimes called "Big John," is the world's sixth tallest building and, unlike the other five, offers room at the top for 1,500 residents in a 703-apartment condominium complex.[...]

Most residents are older married couples, younger childless couples or single persons. One estimate is that there are only about three dozen children in the building and only a handful of teen agers.[...]

Apartment owners on the 92nd floor live 1,003 feet 6 inches above Chicago's North Michigan Avenue. Not satisfied with that, according to a story circulating among building residents, one 92nd floor tenant had his floor raised six inches so that, at 1,004 feet above the ground, he can be the "highest living" person in the world.

The residents have superb views of Chicago, of ice-covered Lake Michigan and of airplanes and helicopters passing below room level. But they often call the doorman to ask, "What's the weather doing down there on the ground?" It can be raining or snowing around the top floors and not on the ground. Or, it could be bright and sunny at the top of the Hancock and raining on the city below.

Quite often, clouds cover Chicago at a level partway up the Hancock, leaving residents looking out over the billowy white expanse as if they were riding in an airplane.[...]

"The thing that everyone buys when they move in is a telescope or binoculars," one resident said. [...]

Some residents have seen traffic accidents on the outer drive along Lake Michigan and have been the

"Big John" :
Chicago's complete city in the sky

An artist's conception of the John Hancock Center in Chicago.

first to call police and ambulances. [...]

Living in a high-rise building removes one from the aspects of nature that can be heard, touched and smelled, but it may bring urban dwellers visually closer to nature.

All the residents interviewed talked about how much time they spent looking at the spectacular views from their windows — at the changing colors of the great lake, at winter sunrises over its ice, at the seasonal march of the sunset around the western horizon, at snowstorms, at the lights of the city and, most dramatically, at the great lightning storms which periodically crash down upon this flat land. [...]

Residents are happy to live above some of the world's hassles — where all the debris goes down the incinerator chute for someone else to worry about and where one calls the management when the heat isn't just right. [...]

Most residents are enthusiastic about living above the city's noise, its bitterly cold winters, its hustle and its crime. "I feel very secure up here. It's like I'm in the womb. I feel very safe," said Barbara Mills.

Those who feel safest and warmest are the several dozen residents who live in the building and work there as well. [...] They are the modern equivalent of those city dwellers who once "lived above the store". [...]

"I drink my last leisurely cup of coffee in the morning before I take the elevator to work, I look out the window and see all the traffic coming in, jammed bumper to bumper. It's a lot more relaxing to live here. You have more time to do what you want to do in life," said one older resident.

Bryce Nelson,
International Herald Tribune,
Feb. 4 1977

---

1. John Hancock: American statesman, first signatory of the Declaration of Independence.

A. UNDERSTANDING VOCABULARY IN CONTEXT/DISCUSSION. You might not understand the meaning of some of the words or expressions that you just read. Work in groups and try to figure out the meaning of these words using information from the reading or your own experience.

high-rise (paragraph 2)
a handful of teenagers (paragraph 4)
superb (paragraph 6)
hassles (paragraph 12)
womb (paragraph 13)

B. LOCATING SPECIFIC INFORMATION. Look for information in the reading that proves or disproves the following statements. If you find the information, write *T* for true or *F* for false. If you cannot find the information, write *DS* for doesn't say.

_____ 1. Thomas James is afraid to go outside.

_____ 2. Thomas James is married.

_____ 3. All six of the world's tallest buildings have apartments at the top.

_____ 4. All six of the world's tallest buildings are in the United States.

_____ 5. There are more children than teenagers living at the John Hancock Center.

_____ 6. The apartments at the center are expensive.

_____ 7. The author has seen the apartment of the tenant who raised her floor six inches.

_____ 8. Sometimes residents can see as far as Lake Erie.

_____ 9. There is a doorman on each floor of the building.

_____ 10. Some of the residents live above the clouds.

_____ 11. Some residents have lots of plants in their apartments so they feel closer to nature.

_____ **12.** Most residents find they have no contact with nature because they live so high up.

_____ **13.** Some residents are a little afraid of living up so high.

_____ **14.** Most of the people who live in the center also work here.

C. COMPOSITION/DISCUSSION. Would you like to live in "Big John"? Why or why not? Make a list of the reasons for and against living in such a building. Then write a composition or discuss your point of view.

VI. Social Scenes

A TEENAGER LOOKS FOR WORK

An interview with Berri Brown, 18, living in St Louis, Missouri.

INTERVIEWER : Do you think it is easy for a teenager to find work ?

BERRI : No. You don't have experience and usually companies want people with experience. A lot of times you're not old enough for the job, mature enough. Then there's the problem of transportation. They always ask for transportation. They want to make sure that you can get to work on time and consistently. And also, that you 5 don't have to rely on your parents to drive you to work.

INTERVIEWER : Do you think it is important for a teenager to work ?

BERRI : Yes, There's lots of reasons why. For me, I think young people should work at a variety of jobs.

INTERVIEWER : To get money ? 10

BERRI : No, for experience. Say, if you have worked waiting on people then you know how to treat people who are waiting on you.

INTERVIEWER : What else do you mean by experience ?

BERRI : Well, you can get a better job afterwards.

INTERVIEWER : Were you able to get a better job once you started working ? 15

BERRI : No, there aren't so many jobs available.

INTERVIEWER : How old were you when you first started working ?

BERRI : About 13 to 14. I worked in the Poppycock Restaurant when my cousin, who owned it, was pregnant. But I didn't get paid.

INTERVIEWER : What did you do ? 20

BERRI : I was a waitress, dishwasher. It was a counter type job and I did almost everything.

INTERVIEWER : Did you like it ?

BERRI : It was work, but I enjoyed serving people. You get to meet a lot of different people.

INTERVIEWER : What other jobs have you had ? 25

BERRI : I was a lab technician and a salesgirl.

INTERVIEWER : Do you think these jobs will help you in what you want to do later on in life ?

BERRI : Yes and no. Yes, in that I feel I have more understanding of other people's jobs. No, in that my jobs were not really involved in what I wanted to do. I wanted to do 30 saleswork because I wanted to learn about fashion, but I never got to sell clothes. I never seem to get the right kind of job. Yet my girlfriend, Debbie, could always get a job even if she was fired, the next day she could get something else.

INTERVIEWER : Why do you think she was different ?

BERRI : Well, for one thing she has the clothes to wear for a sales job and the looks. 35 There's a lot of discrimination, not only in color, just sheer looks. If you look elegant you can get an elegant job.

INTERVIEWER : But can't you always look elegant, even if it is just for the interview ?

BERRI : Not if you don't have the clothes or the know-how.

INTERVIEWER : What do you mean ? 40

BERRI : If no one around you dresses elegantly then you have no model and you have only magazines to look at. And in magazines you just see models and most people aren't. You see jeans outfits that cost $100 just to put together.

INTERVIEWER : Do you worry about going on interviews ?

BERRI : Yeah ! I hate interviews. They are not really interested in what you know; it's your 45 age, your looks, your dress, and like I said who you know; also luck.

INTERVIEWER : How do you feel after your interviews, if you didn't get the job ?

BERRI : Well, the first time it's O.K., the second time you feel bad and then you start getting down. It's degrading and negative to be turned down.

INTERVIEWER : What would your parents say ? 50

BERRI : That's also what used to get me down. Everytime I'd come home Dad would ask me: How did it go ? What did they say ? Do you think you'll get it ?

INTERVIEWER : Wasn't he just trying to be interested and helpful ?

BERRI : Yes, and he's right. But when you've finished a day full of interviews and he's questioning you too, it makes you insecure. You start wondering, did I really do my 55 best, did I show enough self-confidence. Sometimes I'd just get so frustrated that I'd start crying.

A. UNDERSTANDING VOCABULARY IN CONTEXT. Circle the correct answer.

1. In line 5 *consistently* means

   a. everyday.
   b. quickly.

2. In line 35 *the looks* means

   a. she looks intelligent.
   b. she looks pretty.

3. In line 49 *getting down* means

   a. not going to interviews.
   b. feeling depressed.

4. In line 49 *be turned down* means

   a. not get the job.
   b. feel depressed.

B. COMPOSITION/DISCUSSION. Working in groups, list the advantages and disadvantages of working when you're a teenager. Base your list on the reading and your own experience. Then write a composition or discuss your point of view.

C. DEBATE

Young people should work even if they don't need the money because it gives them good life experience.

"I like your looks, Ramsey. You're hired."

KIDS' COUNTRY

Children are a relatively modern invention. Until a few hundred years ago they did not exist. In medieval and Renaissance painting you see pint-sized men and women, wearing grownup clothes and grown-up expressions, performing grown-up tasks. Children did not exist because the family as we know it had not evolved.

Children today not only exist; they have taken over, in no place more than in America, and at no time more than now. It is always Kids' Country here. Our civilization is child-centered, childobsessed. A kid's body is our physical ideal. Plastic surgeons scissor and tuck up. New hair sprouts, transplanted, on wisdom's brow. One way or another we are determined to "keep in shape", and invariably this means keeping a kid's shape. In Kids' Country we do not permit middle-

age. Thirty is promoted over 50, but 30 knows that soon his time to be overtaken will come. In our over-sixty population there are ten widows for every man. Like a child's room, Kids' Country is a mess. New York City seems about to disappear under its load of litter, graffiti and dog-droppings. How is it that China can eliminate the house-fly, and we can't even clean up Central Park?

We are the first society in which parents expect to learn from their children. Such a topsy-turvy situation has come about at least in part because, unlike the rest of the world, ours is an immigrant society, and for immigrants the *only* hope is in the kids. In the Old Country[1], hope was in the father, and how much wealth he could accumulate and pass along to his children. In the growth pattern of America and its ever-expanding frontier, the young man was ever

advised to GO WEST; the father was ever inheriting from his son. Kids' Country may be the inevitable result.

Kids' Country is not all bad. America is the greatest country in the world to grow up in *because* it is Kids' Country. We not only wear kids' clothes and eat kids' food; we dream kids' dreams and make them come true. It was, after all, a boys' game to go to the moon.

But what we are experiencing now seems in many ways the exact opposite of medieval and Renaissance life. If in the old days children did not exist, it seems equally true today that adults, as a class, have begun to disappear, condemning all of us to remain boys and girls forever, jogging and doing push-ups against eternity.

Shana Alexander: *Newsweek*

---

1. Old Country: Europe.

A. UNDERSTANDING VOCABULARY IN CONTEXT/DISCUSSION.

You might not understand the meaning of some of the words or expressions that you just read. Work in groups and try to figure out the meaning of these words using information from the reading or your own experience.

pint-sized (paragraph 1)
tuck up (paragraph 2)
on wisdom's brow (paragraph 2)
"keep in shape" (paragraph 2)

topsy-turvy (paragraph 3)
jogging (last paragraph)
push-ups (last paragraph)

B. UNDERSTANDING THE AUTHOR'S PURPOSE.

Circle the correct answer.

1. In paragraph 1 the author uses the example of the Renaissance painting to show that

   a. adults were smaller and thinner at that time, but they still had lots of work to do.
   b. children looked and acted like adults at that time.
   c. children were not permitted to appear in family paintings at that time.

2. According to the author, what is the reason that *in our over-sixty population there are ten widows for every man?* (paragraph 2)

   a. Men exercise too hard because they want to stay young.
   b. Men work too hard.
   c. The author doesn't clearly state the reason.

3. The author mentions that *New York City seems about to disappear under its load of litter, graffiti and dog-droppings* (paragraph 2) because she wants to show

   a. that New York City is overpopulated.
   b. how childish and irresponsible people are.
   c. how difficult life is today.

4. In paragraph 3 *the Old Country* is contrasted with America

   a. to show differences in family size.
   b. to show two kinds of geography.
   c. to show two different kinds of economic relations between generations.

5. In paragraph 4 going to the moon is an example of

   a. America's dreams and creativity.
   b. America's childish and irresponsible behavior.
   c. why America hasn't grown up.

6. When the author says *condemning all of us to remain boys and girls forever, jogging and doing push-ups against eternity* (paragraph 5), she is

   a. saying that she thinks people shouldn't be so concerned about physical fitness.
   b. complaining that she feels too old and tired to do such hard exercise.
   c. criticizing American society for its overemphasis on youth and physical appearance.

C. DEBATE

The older you get the wiser you are.

MAKING A FUTURE

Biff and Happy, the two sons of a traveling salesman, are home again together on a visit, and exchange reflexions before going to sleep in the old room they shared while they were living with their parents.

HAPPY

But I think if you just got started — I mean — is there any future for you out there?

BIFF

I tell ya, Hap, I don't know what the future is. I don't know — what I'm supposed to want.

HAPPY

What do you mean?

BIFF

Well, I spent six or seven years after high school trying to work myself up. Shipping clerk, salesman, business of one kind or another. And it's a measly manner of existence. To get on that subway on the hot mornings in summer. To devote your whole life to keeping stock, or making phone calls, or selling or buying. To suffer fifty weeks of the year for the sake of a two-week vacation, when all you really desire is to be outdoors, with your shirt off. And always to have to get ahead of the next fella. And still — that's how you build a future.

HAPPY

Well, you really enjoy it on a farm? Are you content out there?

BIFF *(with rising agitation)*

Hap, I've had twenty or thirty different kinds of jobs since I left home before the war, and it always turns out the same. I just realized it lately. In Nebraska when I herded cattle, and the Dakotas, and Arizona, and now in Texas. It's why I came home now, I guess, because I realized it. This farm I work on, it's spring there now, see? And they've got about fifteen new colts. There's nothing more inspiring or — beautiful — than the sight of a mare and a new colt. And it's cool there now, see? Texas is cool now, and it's spring. And whenever spring comes to where I am, I suddenly get the feeling, my God, I'm not getting anywhere! What the hell am I doing, playing around with horses, twenty-eight dollars a week! I'm thirty-four years old, I oughta be makin' my future. That's when I come running home. And now, I get here, and I don't know what to do with myself. *(After a pause)* I've always made a point of not wasting my life, and every time I come back here I know that all I've done is to waste my life.

HAPPY

You're a poet, you know that, Biff? You're a — you're an idealist!

BIFF

No, I'm mixed up very bad.

Arthur Miller: *Death of a Salesman*

B. DISCUSSION. Discuss the answers to the questions in Exercise A in groups.

C. LOCATING SPECIFIC INFORMATION. Read the passage again and write the statements that tell the reader

1. that Biff would rather work outside. _____

_____

2. where Biff is working right now. _____

_____

3. what time of year it is when Biff and Happy are talking. _____

_____

D. INFERRING MEANING/DISCUSSION. Circle the answer that you think describes Happy in the conversation. Discuss your answers in groups.

   a. He is trying to be sympathetic.
   b. He is critical of his brother's life style.
   c. He is trying to give his brother some suggestions.

E. DEBATE

It is better to live in the present and enjoy it than build a future.

The Terrible People

A. READING WITH A PURPOSE. Read only as far as necessary to complete this statement:

According to the author, "The Terrible People" are
a. poor people.
b. uneducated people.
c. rich people.

Where did you find the answer?   Line _____ .

People who have what they want are very fond of telling people who haven't what
    they want that they really don't want it.
And I wish I could afford to gather all such people into a gloomy castle on the
    Danube and hire half a dozen capable Draculas to haunt it.
I don't mind their having a lot of money, and I don't care how they employ it.   5
But I do think that they damn well ought to admit they enjoy it.
But no, they insist on being stealthy
About the pleasures of being wealthy,
And the possession of a handsome annuity
Makes them think that to say how hard it is to make both ends meet is their bounden   10
    duity.
You cannot conceive of an occasion
Which will find them without some subtle evasion.
Yes indeed, with arguments they are very fecund;
Their first point is that money isn't everything, and that they have no money anyhow   15
    is their second.
Some people's money is merited,
And other people's is inherited.
But wherever it comes from,
They talk about it as if it were something you got pink gums from.   20
This may well be,
But if so, why do they not relieve themselves of the burden by transferring it to the
    deserving poor or to me?
Perhaps indeed the possession of wealth is constantly distressing,
But I should be quite willing to assume every curse of wealth if I could at the same   25
    time assume every blessing.
The only incurable troubles of the rich are the troubles that money can't cure,
Which is a kind of trouble that is even more troublesome if you are poor.
Certainly there are lots of things in life that money won't buy, but it's very funny —   30
Have you ever tried to buy them without money?

Ogden Nash: *The Terrible People*

B. UNDERSTANDING THE MAIN IDEA. Check the correct answer.

This author

_____ **1.** doesn't like rich people because he thinks it's immoral to have so much money.

_____ **2.** thinks rich people spend their money in very foolish ways.

_____ **3.** thinks rich people should be honest and admit that it's very nice to have money.

_____ **4.** thinks that rich people would feel better if they gave some of their money to the poor.

_____ **5.** thinks that rich people have more troubles than poor people.

C. UNDERSTANDING VOCABULARY IN CONTEXT. Fill in the blanks with words from the text.

1. The author thinks that rich people are _____ (line 7) because they won't say they like having money.

2. Another way of saying that someone has a lot of money is to say they have _____ _____. (line 9)

3. Find an expression in line 10 that means "to have enough money to pay their bills."

_____

4. Find a word in line 22 that means "something that is difficult or causes problems."

_____

5. The opposite of a *curse of wealth* (line 25) is a _____. (line 26)

6. Troubles that can't be cured (line 27) are _____troubles. (line 27)

D. DISCUSSION. The poem suggests that wealthy people do not like to admit they enjoy being rich. Do you think that this is true?

John Wayne in *Rio Bravo* by H. Hawks.

HOLLYWOOD, HOLLYWOOD

By the end of the thirties, Hollywood had tested, refined and codified the money-making formula on the basis of which most of its successful films have since been made. All the different types of films associated with Hollywood had emerged: the back-stage musical, the screwball comedy, the gangster story, the costume drama, the Western, the tearjerker, the suspense-thriller, the confessional tale, the 5
knockabout farce, the semi-historical biography, the pseudo-classic and the Walt Disney animated cartoon. These were the staple items on the Hollywood menu, and by and large they have remained so to the present day. The most solidly satisfying and the most truly American of these is the Western. [...]

There has never been a period when the Western was totally out. Its popularity 10
seems to be constant. There are several possible explanations of why this should be so: nostalgia for a way of life that was free and unhampered by the ties and restrictions of "civilised" behavior, the pride of a sedentary American society in the physical prowess, capacity for endurance and sheer guts of their forebears. [...] And, of course, the Western enjoys the advantage of being able to crystallise its 15

Georges Guétary in *An American in Paris* by V. Minelli.

moral [and other] conflicts in a simple and exciting situation: two men facing each other with guns in their hands. In no other kind of drama can latent feelings be so easily made overt. [...]

Next to the Western, the film most readily associated with Hollywood is the musical. At its best it owes little to the operetta or the musical comedy from which it has evolved. [...] As the musical became established as a sure-fire box-office attraction, it resorted increasingly to the most banal plot of all: the back-stage story of the rise to fame and wealth of a simple chorus girl. There were innumerable and indistinguishable variations [...] on this theme and they made the Hollywood musical a pejorative term for many years. [...] Vincente Minelli [and others] freed the musical from the too-familiar back-stage milieu, from the need to contrive "natural" opportunities for the characters to burst into song, and from show biz sentimentality. Instead [...] directors permitted their characters to sing in the streets of New York [...], on the Empire State building, in subways; song and music became an integral part of the story, advancing the action and the development of the characters.[...]

The animated cartoon film is also very much a product of Hollywood. As a popular way of story-telling, the cartoon owes its existence entirely to Walt Disney who, on this score, must be regarded as one of the great innovators of the cinema.

Bambi by Walt Disney.

The first Mickey Mouse adventure appeared in 1928 and was an immediate success. 35
In the next three years, Disney turned out ninety of these short features and in
them his inventiveness, his ingenuity and his sense of fantasy grew and developed
amazingly. With his first full length feature, *Snow White and the Seven Dwarfs*
(1938), it seemed that the cinema might have found its purest artist: all the
grotesque characters of the story were magnificently realised by Disney's 40
draughtsmen under the supervision of the maestro: and the story was unfolded with
much imagination and many inspired touches. But the most daring use of the
medium was *Fantasia* (1940), an abstract film in which Disney sought to provide the
visual equivalent to classical music. Up to this stage, Disney was still developing:
and though he did not actually do any of the drawing in his films, they were his 45
conceptions.[...]

The achievements of the commercial cinema came to a climax in 1939 when David
O. Selznick produced *Gone With The Wind,* which might be described as the
apotheosis of the Hollywood film. It was the longest novelette ever made (running
three hours and forty minutes) and had, as they say, "everything": a beautiful self- 50
centered heroine (Vivien Leigh) who suffered the whole range of emotional
upheavals; a roguish hero (Clark Gable), rough in manner but strong and
resourceful in moments of crisis; a gentle and gentlemanly second-lead (Leslie
Howard); a good woman (Olivia de Havilland) who nearly dies in childbirth; the
American Civil War; attempted rape; marital strife; crimson sunsets; a doctor who 55
has to operate without chloroform; a hero who carries his struggling wife up the
grand-staircase; a pregnant heroine who falls down the grand-staircase; the decline
and decay of the South; the prostitute with a heart of gold; the scoundrel who
becomes a millionaire. What more could anyone want? What more could anyone
conceivably be given? It made a fortune. Some years later, on being reissued again 60
and despite our present familiarity with the epic, it was still highly successful.

Thomas Wiseman : *Cinema*

Vivian Leigh in *Gone With The Wind* by V. Fleming.

A. UNDERSTANDING VOCABULARY IN CONTEXT. Circle the correct answer.

1. A *screwball comedy* (paragraph 1) is probably

    a. a crazy comedy.
    b. a sports comedy.

2. A *tearjerker* (paragraph 1) is probably

    a. a movie with a lot of action.
    b. a sad movie.

3. A *knockabout farce* (paragraph 1) is probably

    a. a story about fighters.
    b. a rough comedy.

4. *Sheer guts* (paragraph 2) probably means

    a. courage.
    b. size.

5. A *sure-fire box-office attraction* (paragraph 3) is probably

    a. a movie that is sure to make a lot of money.
    b. a movie that may or may not make a lot of money.

6. A *banal* plot (paragraph 3) is probably

    a. original and unusual.
    b. not original or unusual.

7. A *pejorative term* (paragraph 3) is probably

    a. a negative term.
    b. a positive term.

8. *Short features* (paragraph 4) are probably

    a cartoons that last a short time.
    b. small cartoon characters, e.g., Mickey Mouse.

9. An *apotheosis* (paragraph 5) is probably

    a. something that's very good.
    b. something that's very expensive.

10. *Marital strife* (paragraph 5) probably means

    a. lots of weddings.
    b. problems within marriages.

B. **DISCUSSION.** What is the "formula" for a successful film today? Look at the movie page of a current newspaper. Which of the films do you think will be the most successful?

"Now in this scene, Franz Schubert, the composer, falls asleep and dreams his melody while the girls dance it out on the piano keys. Get it?"

Drawing by Carl Rose: ©1935, 1963. The New Yorker Magazine, Inc.

Some blue jeans wearers . . .

Blue Jeans Culture

The idea that he might one day be hailed as a world fashion leader would surely have given old Levi Strauss a hearty laugh. His famous pants had started out as a roll of tent canvas which he hoped to peddle to prospectors on his arrival in California in 1850. Company legend has it that a miner greeted young Strauss with the news that he should have brought pants instead of tent material on the long trip from New York. "Pants don't hold up worth a hoot in the diggings," the miner said, at which point Strauss beat a path to the nearest tailor and ordered more cloth from his brothers in New York. They sent him the now-familiar tough cotton fabric from France, and the miners started pouring into Strauss's store to plop down a dollar for a pair of "Levi's pants."

Last year, denim enthusiasts the world over paid $405 million for assorted Levi products, including 75 million pairs of pants, a figure which makes Levi Strauss the world's No 1 pants-maker. American students have been known to finance their entire summer European travels by selling off extra Levi's, and in Russia a pair with the leather logo patch intact can fetch $90 in the black market. Levi's have been ensconced in the Smithsonian[1] and presented a special Coty Award as America's most significant contribution to international fashion.

As a measure of flattery, Levi's have been imitated and copied — illegally — more than any other piece of clothing. They are shipped through Europe in plain brown boxes to avoid theft. Despite trademark registration in more than 50 countries, the company uncovered at least 50 counterfeit "Levi" models last year. The official Levi tag now goes on more than 2,000 items ranging from plush corduroy pants to handbags, notebooks and theater seats. But the keystone of the company's operations is still the basic blue-denim jeans, which have remained virtually unchanged for 122 years. The only alterations in design have been a slight modification of the copper rivets on seams, changing the rear patch from real leather to one of synthetic material (a decision which required a board of directors' meeting) and removing the crotch rivet, an instant decision made when a former company president, Walter Haas, once stood too long near a blazing campfire.

From *Life Magazine*, Nov 24, 1972

---

1. the Smithsonian (Institution): the national museum of science and industry in Washington, D.C.

A. **INFERRING MEANING.** Write *T* for true or *F* for false.

_____ 1. Levi Strauss made the pants himself.

_____ 2. Levi's brothers sent him the pants from New York.

_____ 3. Denim is a type of cotton.

_____ 4. In Russia it is difficult to find Levi's in department stores.

_____ 5. A trademark registration is a way of protecting a product.

_____ 6. "Levi" is a trademark.

_____ 7. A rivet is made of metal.

_____ 8. The crotch rivet was the rivet that went between the legs on the jeans.

B. **DISCUSSION.** Why do you think so many people wear blue jeans?

By permission of Johnny Hart and Field Enterprises, Inc.

CAR CULTURE

A. PREDICTING. Read only the first paragraph of this article. What do you think the rest of the reading will be about?

1. Ernest Dichter's research.
2. Why the automobile is so important in modern society.
3. Procedures for getting a license.
4. New developments in the automotive industry.

A modern sculpture in Texas.

Motivational researcher Ernest Dichter [...] is shrewdly insightful when he suggests that the auto is the "most powerful tool for mastery" available to the ordinary Western man. "The automobile has become the modern symbol of initiation. The license of the sixteen-year-old is a valid admission to adult society."

In the affluent nations, he writes, "most people have enough to eat and are reasonably well housed. Having achieved this thousand-year-old dream of humanity, they now reach out for further satisfactions. They want to travel, discover, be at least physically independent. The automobile is the modern symbol of mobility…" In fact, the last thing that any family wishes to surrender, when hardpressed by financial hardship, is the automobile, and the worst punishment an American parent can mete out to a teenager is to "ground" him—i.e., to deprive him of the use of an automobile.

Young girls in the United States, when asked what they regard as important about a boy, immediately list a car. Sixty-seven percent of those interviewed in a recent survey said a car is "essential", and a nineteen-year-old boy, Alfred Uranga of Albuquerque, N.M.[1], confirmed gloomily that "If a guy doesn't have a car, he doesn't have a girl". Just how deep this passion for automobility runs among the youth is tragically illustrated by the suicide of a seventeen-year-old Wisconsin boy, William Nebel, who was "grounded" by his father after his driver's license was suspended for speeding. Before putting a .22 caliber rifle bullet in his brain, the boy penned a note that ended, "Without a license, I don't have my car, job or social life. So I think that it is better to end it all right now." It is clear that millions of young people all over the technological world agree with the poet Marinetti who, more than half a century ago, shouted: "A roaring racing car [...] is more beautiful than the Winged Victory."

Alvin Toffler: Future Shock

1. N.M.: New Mexico.

B. DISCUSSING YOUR PREDICTION. Was your prediction correct?

C. UNDERSTANDING THE MAIN IDEA. Circle the correct answer.

1. The main idea in paragraph 2 is that

   a. most people today have enough to eat and are well housed.
   b. the worst punishment for a teenager is to "ground" him.
   c. the automobile is central to modern American life.

2. The main idea of paragraph 3 is that

   a. a roaring racing car is more beautiful than Winged Victory.
   b. William Nebel killed himself.
   c. teenagers in the United States think that a car is essential.

D. DISCUSSION. To what extent are cars a necessary part of life in your country?

Stove with Meats by Claes Oldenburg, 1961.

What Is Art ?

A sad-eyed man of fifty-two, Kraushar met me at his modern house in Lawrence, Long Island. He said that he had never collected anything of any kind, nor did he know anything about art, until he saw a Lichtenstein[1] in the fall of 1961. "I couldn't get it out of my mind," he told me. Since that pivotal day he has bought well over a hundred works, and every one of them is pop art.

"As far as I'm concerned, there is no other art," Kraushar said. "The other stuff is all history."[...]

I noticed that the centerpiece on the table was an Oldenburg[1] baked potato, split open with a dab of butter on top. "It's as appropriate as anything you'd want to have," Kraushar said.

Then I noticed that this wasn't the only food. All the pop art in the dining room was food, most of it by Oldenburg. A plate of soup, a dish of crackers and a piece of cheesecake were on one shelf, and on the wall above it hung a five-foot slab of meat and six Good Humor[2] bars. Elsewhere was a crate of apples and pears by Robert Watts[1] and a Warhol[1] canvas absolutely depicting one hundred cans of Campbell's[3] beef noodle broth. I began to feel slightly sick; I couldn't even imagine a meal amid all that appropriate art.

But at least I knew it was art. In the kitchen I completely lost the ability to tell which was food and which was sculpture. The first thing I saw on a counter was a box of eggs and a half-eaten ham. The eggs were obviously real and the ham was unquestionably art — in fact, I thought that the artist (was it Oldenburg?) had made a particularly good composition of the gravy and the left-over bits.

"Those eggs are by Watts," Kraushar said.

"And who did the ham?" I asked.

"Nobody," he said. I smelled the ham, and to my amazement it was ham. Mrs Kraushar came in to put some groceries away. I didn't envy her — the kitchen was full of illusions. Realistic paintings of food hung over tables that held artistic baskets of fruit.

Along one wall was a long white meat counter, of the kind used in supermarkets, and it was full of frozen steaks and chops, real enough to eat. Then I recognized it as the central piece in the famous "supermarket" show that I had seen earlier at the Bianchini Gallery, which consisted entirely of pop art foods. I had wondered at the time who would buy this disquieting piece — probably no other work in the pop movement has so baldly asked the question "what is art?" — and would take it home. Now I knew. I also knew

that the Kraushar's kitchen was no place for a careless guest to go browsing for a midnight snack.[...]

And so the trail went winding on, as I left Kraushar's house, from room to room, through foyers and alcoves and lavatories and nooks, down corridors lined with smaller paintings, past tables that held what appeared to be shopping bags and pin boxes and other everyday objects but which, in fact, were artists' renditions of shopping bags and pin boxes and other everyday objects. It was pop art pure and rampant, uncrossed with any other strain from art's long lineage, unrelieved by subtlely or suggestion. And surely there is nothing else like it in the world.[...]

And woe to the visitor who doesn't know what the truly great art of today is. "I'm much too devoted to the pieces to have them ridiculed," Kraushar said. "There are certain people that I have to tell in advance what sort of things they'll find if they come to see me. I say to them, 'The only reason you'll know they're art is because they're in my house.'"

William K. Zinsser : *Pop Goes America*

---

1. Lichtenstein, Oldenburg, Watts, Warhol: world-famous contemporary American artists. 2. Good Humor: a brand of ice cream. 3. Campbell: a brand of canned soups.

A. UNDERSTANDING THE AUTHOR'S PURPOSE. Circle the correct answer.

1. The author says that Kraushar doesn't know about any other art besides pop art (paragraph 1) so that

   a. we feel sorry for Kraushar.
   b. we will realize that Kraushar is not very knowledgeable about art.

2. When the author says, "I couldn't even imagine a meal amid all that appropriate art" (paragraph 4),

   a. he is being truthful. He thinks that the art is appropriate, but he doesn't feel well.
   b. he is being ironic. He doesn't think the art is appropriate.

3. When the author says, ". . . to my amazement it was ham" (paragraph 8),

   a. he is exaggerating to be funny.
   b. he wants us to know that he was very surprised.

4. When the author says, ''I also knew that the Kraushars' kitchen was no place for a careless guest to go browsing for a midnight snack'' (paragraph 9), he is

    a. praising the painting on the wall because it looks so real.
    b. being funny.

5. When the author says, ''And surely there is nothing else like it in the world'' (paragraph 10), he is

    a. describing pop art.
    b. praising pop art.

6. When Krausher says, ''The only reason you'll know they're art is because they're in my house'' (last paragraph),

    a. he convinces people that pop art is real art.
    b. he doesn't convince people that pop art is real art.

B. DISCUSSION. What is the author's opinion of pop art? Why do you think ''What is Art?'' is the title of this reading?

BIOGRAPHICAL NOTES

BIRD, Caroline (1915–   )
Former editor and professor, Bird is best known for her works of nonfiction including *Everything a Woman Needs to Know to Get Paid What She's Worth* (1973), *The Case Against College* (1975), *Enterprising Women* (1976) and *The Two Paycheck Marriage* (1979). She has also published articles in national magazines.

BUCHWALD, Art (1925–   )
A well-known contemporary humorist, Buchwald's columns in the *International Herald Tribune* are syndicated to a large number of newspapers throughout the United States to the delight of millions of readers.

CAPOTE, Truman (1924–   )
A remarkable stylist and a New York socialite, Capote had published several collections of short stories, including *Breakfast at Tiffany's* (1958), when he produced *In Cold Blood* in 1966. The book sold some three million copies and was later made into a movie. Capote has written a number of television plays since then, and in 1980 he published a collection of short stories entitled *Music for Chameleons*.

DOCTOROW, E. L. (1931–   )
A novelist who was born in New York and educated at Kenyon College and Columbia University, Doctorow's works include *Welcome to Hard Times* (1976), *The Book of Daniel* (1971), *Ragtime* (1975) and *Loon Lake* (1980). *Ragtime* was released as a film in 1981.

DOS PASSOS, John (1896–1970)
A novelist who came to prominence with *Manhattan Transfer* (1925), Dos Passos developed a literary style that was revolutionary in its combination of naturalism and stream-of-consciousness techniques. A portrayal in hundreds of brief episodes of the many-faceted life of New York City, the book reflected his concern for individual liberty and his social conscience. His major work, the trilogy *U.S.A.* (1938), is a panorama of American life, comprising *The 42nd Parallel* (1930), *1919* (1932) and *The Big Money* (1936).

EMERSON, Ralph Waldo (1803–1882)
A New England essayist and poet, Emerson became the central figure of the Transcendentalist spirit of intellectual independence from all obstacles to originality. Through his lectures and writings he exerted a strong and long-lasting influence on American philosophy.

GIOVANNI, Nikki (1943–   )
Poet, writer and lecturer, Giovanni was born in Knoxville, Tennessee, and educated at Fisk University. Explicitly concerned with the black revolution, she has been very outspoken on the problems of the black woman. Her recent publications include *Cotton Candy on a Rainy Day* (1980) and *Vacation Time: Poems for Children* (1981).

HAILEY, Arthur (1920–   )
Novelist and playwright, Hailey was born in Luton, England, emigrated to Canada in 1947 and became a full-time writer in 1956. His first success was the television play, *Flight into Danger*. His outstandingly successful novels include *In High Places* (1961), *Hotel* (1965), *Airport* (1968), *Wheels* (1971), *The Moneychangers* (1975) and *Overload* (1979). A number of Hailey's stories have been made into movies.

HALEY, Alex (1921–   )
Journalist and author, Haley retired from the U.S. Coast Guard in 1959 after twenty years of service in order to write. His first book, *The Autobiography of Malcolm X*, was a major critical success. It was while he was working as a writer and interviewer for *Playboy* that Haley began researching and writing *Roots* (1977), a project which took twelve years of work. Two television specials, *Roots* and *Roots: The Next Generation*, were based on this best-seller.

KEROUAC, Jack (1922–1969)
Novelist and poet, Kerouac is recognized as the leading representative of the beatnik subculture. Born in Lowell, Massachusetts, in a French-speaking family of Canadian origin, Kerouac did a variety of casual jobs before entering Columbia where he met poets and intellectuals such as Allen Ginsberg and Neal Cassady. From 1943 to 1950 he roamed through the United States and Mexico. *On the Road,* his most famous novel, was written during a frantic three weeks in 1951, the first of a series published in quick succession.

KING, Martin Luther, Jr. (1929–1968)
A Baptist pastor in Montgomery, Alabama, King came into public view in 1955 when he led a successful boycott by the black community of Montgomery's segregated buses, which led to the Supreme Court's ruling against racial discrimination in transportation. Elected president of the Southern Christian Leadership Conference in 1957, he developed a nonviolent but active strategy of massive confrontation against injustice, which climaxed in the March on Washington in 1963. Later criticized by more militant black activists, he was awarded the Nobel Peace Prize in 1964. He was shot to death by a sniper in Memphis in 1968.

KRUTCH, Joseph Wood (1893–1970)
Critic for *The Nation*, essayist and teacher, it was Krutch's career as a naturalist that gained him his greatest fame. He left his post at Columbia University in 1952 and moved to the Tucson, Arizona, area to live in an adobe house in the desert. Most of his later books express his deep concern with and affection for the natural world and are eloquent pleas for a sane relationship between man and nature.

LINCOLN, Abraham (1809–1865)
Born in a log cabin in Kentucky, Lincoln grew up in the poverty of a frontier family to become the sixteenth president of the United States in March 1861. His election triggered the secession of seven Southern states, and the Civil War broke out in April 1861. Reelected by a large majority in 1864, he was shot while attending a theater performance only three days after General Lee's surrender at Appomattox.

MILLER, Arthur (1915–)
Playwright and author, Miller was raised in modest circumstances and had to work full-time while studying to finance his university degree. His first successful play, *All My Sons*, was performed in 1947, and *Death of a Salesman* followed in 1949. Miller's account of the Salem witch trials in *The Crucible* (1953) closely paralleled political events of the McCarthy anti-Communist crusade. Other plays include *A View from the Bridge* (1955), *After the Fall* (1964), *The Price* (1968) and the screenplay for *The Misfits* (1961), in which the lead female role was played by Marilyn Monroe. Miller and Monroe were ·married in 1956 and divorced in 1960. In 1978 a collection of essays, *The Theater Essays of Arthur Miller*, was published.

NASH, Ogden (1902–1971)
A writer of light verse, Nash is known for his sophisticated whimsy, use of the pun and distorted rhyme, and the cleverness of his free-verse style. Nash left teaching after one year because he was being harrassed by his fourteen-year-old students and began contributing his verse to various magazines. Much of his writing has appeared in the *New Yorker*. His best known collections of verse are probably *The Face is Familiar* (1940), *Parents Keep Out* (1951) and *You Can't Get There From Here* (1957).

STEINBECK, John (1902–1968)
A highly successful novelist and short-story writer of proletarian sympathies, Steinbeck was born in Salinas, California. He is noted for his realistic studies of life among the depressed economic classes of the United States, especially the itinerant farm laborers of California. His books include *Tortilla Flat* (1935), *Cannery Row* (1945), *In Dubious Battle* (1979), *Of Mice and Men* (1937), *The Grapes of Wrath* (1939) and *East of Eden* (1952). In 1940 he was awarded the Pulitzer Prize and in 1962 the Nobel Prize for Literature. *Travels With Charley* (1962) is the account of his trip across the United States in the company of an elderly poodle.

TERKEL, Studs Louis (1912–)
A well-known author of both fiction and nonfiction, Terkel's publications include *Giants of Jazz* (1956), *Amazing Grace* (1959), *Division Street: America* (1966), *Hard Times* (1970), *Working* (1974), *Talking to Myself* (1977) and *American Dream: Lost & Found* (1980). He has also had an extensive career as an actor, interviewer and narrator in theater, television and radio.

TOFFLER, Alvin (1928–)
Former editor of *Fortune* magazine and Washington correspondent, Toffler has become a specialist of the ''sociology of the future.'' He is the author of *The Culture Consumers* (1964), *Future Shock* (1971) and *The Third Wave* (1980), has contributed to numerous periodicals and taught in some of the most prestigious universities in the United States.

WAUGH, Evelyn Arthur St. John (1903–1966)
Satirical novelist and essayist, Waugh was born in London and educated at Lancing and Oxford. He studied art, worked on the *Daily Express* and mixed with high society. *Decline and Fall* (1928), *Scoop* (1938), *Brideshead Revisited* (1945) and *The Loved One* (1948) are among his most famous works. *Brideshead Revisited* has been made into a BBC television production.

ANSWER KEY

For some of the exercises there may be more than one correct answer. If students have answers that are different from the ones provided, they should be able to explain why they answered as they did. Answers are not provided for Discussion, Composition or Debate exercises.

I. THE AMERICAN DREAM . . .

What Does It Mean? *page 4*

A
1. living without hardship
2. that life could be what you made it
3. the American Dream
4. seeing the constant portrayal of the good
5. life in the mass media
6. acquiring more things

B
1. b
2. c
3. a
4. b

C
1. D
2. A
3. D
4. D
5. A
6. A
7. D

Paradox and Dream *page 6*

A
1. a
2. a
3. b
4. b

B
2. . . . it is a rare man or woman who, when the power goes off, knows how to look for a burned-out fuse and replace it. (lines 6-7)
3. There isn't a man among us in ten thousand who knows how to butcher a cow or a pig and cut it up for eating, let alone a wild animal. (lines 10-11)
4. . . . when hunting season opens there is a slaughter of farm animals and humans by men and women who couldn't hit a

real target if they could see it. (lines 12-14)
5. . . . fewer and fewer farmers feed more and more people. (line 15)

I Have a Dream *page 9*

A
1. b
2. a
3. c
4. b

B
2. the Emancipation Proclamation
3. the United States
4. that all men are created equal
5. the United States
6. all of the previous paragraph
7. all people

C
1. A hundred years after the Emancipation Proclamation, the black American is still not free.
2. People will continue to fight for justice no matter what happens.
3. Someday the United States will achieve its ideals.
4. Someday black and white Americans will get together socially.
5. Even Mississippi, one of the worst states, will change.
6. The governor of Alabama is against change.
7. Someday in Alabama, black and white children will play together.
8. I believe that changes will take place everywhere.

A Slice of a Continent *page 13*

A
1. b
2. b
3. b
4. c

Loving America *page 16*

A
1. c
2. b
3. b
4. a
5. b
6. c

B
2. a belief in the innate superiority of their own people
3. democracy, free enterprise, individualism
4. need to believe/ resistance to cynicism restlessness/ refusal to settle for what is
5. disease, poverty
6. the state, the military, the church, scholarship
7. courage, kindness, faith

The Declaration of Independence *page 19*

A
1. c
2. c
3. c

II. . . . REACHING FOR IT

Moving to the Sunbelt *page 22*

A
1. c
2. b
3. a
4. a
5. a
6. a

The Gold Rush *page 24*

A

3
2
4
1

B
2. *F* Had the deluge dropped onto an unprepared California, the results would have been disastrous. Thanks to the continent's width, however, men who were familiar with the West had *a year's grace* . . . (paragraph 1)

3. *F* The alcalde of Monterey described the situation there: *"All were off for the mines, . . ."* (paragraph 2)
4. *F* In mid 1848, California's *non-Indian* population, women and children included, amounted to no more than fourteen thousand. Perhaps *half of these were native Californios . . .* (paragraph 3)
5. *F* Their clamour for supplies sent prices skyrocketing. (paragraph 4)
6. *T* The great *drawback* was a *dearth* of food. (paragraph 5)
7. *T* . . . deposits of gold-bearing gravel called bars. These had formed during high water *wherever the current was slack . . .* (paragraph 6)
8. *F* Receding water opened these spots to the *crude tools* of the early miners. (paragraph 6)
9. *T* . . . *even those unoriginal souls* who clung near the familiar bars at Coloma, the site of Marshall's discovery, are said to have *averaged twenty-five to thirty dollars a day . . .* (last paragraph)
10. *F* Under such conditions, a man did not mind standing in icy water all day while *a hot sun beat on his head, his shoes turned to pulp,* and *his stomach,* assaulted with insufficient amounts of monotonous food, *sent forth calls of distress.* (last paragraph)

C
1. b
2. b
3. a
4. b
5. b
6. b
7. b

One Woman's Empire *page 29*

A 2

B
1. b
2. b
3. a
4. b
5. a
6. b
7. a

8. a
9. a
10. a

From Gadgets to People *page 32*

A

1
3
4
7
9
10
11

Space Hardware Comes to Earth *page 34*

A

1. a
2. c
3. a
4. c

Roots *page 35*

A

1. a
2. b
3. b
4. a
5. a

"We've come a long way, babe!" *page 38*

A

1. b
2. a
3. a
4. b
5. b
6. a
7. b
8. b
9. b

B

1. c
2. a

C

1. b
2. b
3. b
4. a
5. b

Carol *page 42*

B

1. b
2. b
3. b
4. a
5. b

III. THE OTHER SIDE OF THE DREAM

How the Indians Saw It *page 48*

A

1. The Rock River furnished fish, the land produced good crops, the hunting grounds were good.
2. wild, wilderness, infested, savage
3. tame, bountiful, blessings
4. When Indians kill meat, we eat it all up.
   When we dig roots and build houses, we make little holes.
   When we burn grass, we don't ruin things.
   We don't chop down trees.
5. White people plow up the ground, pull down the trees, kill everything, blast rocks.
6. Soon there would be no buffalo on the plains, fewer war parties, almost no raids, white men were on the plains, houses near water holes, villages on the rivers.

Greer County Bachelor *page 51*

A

1. starving to death
2. government claim
3. ragged
4. bedbug, grasshopper, flea
5. blizzards
6. toothless, grey
7. call quits

B

1
3
4
6

1902: They Came to America *page 53*

B

1. a, c, d, e, g, i

2. b, c, f, g

C

1. a
2. a
3. b
4. b
5. b

The History of Pollution *page 56*

A b

C

1. b
2. b
3. a

Daddy, what did you do in the war against pollution? *page 59*

A

1. b
2. a
3. a
4. b
5. a
6. b

Garden City *page 61*

A

1. passing through Garden City
2. living in Garden City
3. everything else a decent man needs
4. a public library, a daily newspaper, shady squares, placid residential streets, a big park, a swimming pool
5. people who have stayed in their home town
6. the people in Garden City
7. businessmen, bankers, lawyers, physicians and prominent ranchers

B

1. b
2. a
3. a
4. a
5. a
6. b

What Men? What Needs? *page 64*

A

1. He hates to think that something he has loved or enjoyed will disappear.
2. The world grows more crowded every year at an ever increasing rate. Men continue destroying nature in their search for resources and space.
3. Public lands were set aside as national parks.
4. Many people wish to develop these natural reserves because they argue that doing so will be more helpful to people and "human needs come first".
5. Someday overpopulation will reach the point where all lands will be filled with people.

Fuel for the future—will America have enough? *page 66*

1. b
2. c, e

IV. THE AMERICAN MOSAIC

The Real America? *page 70*

A

1. the fact that there is an average level of civilization throughout the United States
2. the different countries that people's ancestors come from
3. that there is nothing to see between Denver and Chicago
4. in the United States
5. Indian relations—the fact that Indians have had their land taken away and have been sent to live on reservations
6. the problem with the Indians

C

1. T
2. T
3. F
4. F
5. F
6. F
7. F

Nikki Rosa *page 72*

A
1. b
2. a
3. b
4. b

On the Road *page 73*

A
1. b

C
1. sprawled out
2. bumpkins
3. rotgut
4. drizzling
5. old men
6. bouncing off
7. hobo
8. Where you headed?
9. hobo rags
10. moronically
11. folly
12. dough
13. mulled this over
14. having a hell of a time

San Antonio, Tex. *page 77*

B
1. b
2. a
3. a

C
1. b
2. b
3. a

Big Money, Hard Job *page 79*

A
1. a
2. b
3. b
4. b
5. a
6. b
7. c

V. THE AMERICAN WAY OF LIFE

Living on Credit *page 84*

B
1. without being solicited
2. we got hooked
3. Monopoly money
4. when reality hits you in the face
5. getting in over my head in debt

Plastic World *page 86*

A trash
rubbish
waste
filth
thrown-out things
metal wastes
atomic wastes
chemical wastes
wastes

B
1. b
2. b
3. b
4. a

Perpetual Care *page 89*

A
1. a
2. b
3. a
4. a
5. a
6. b
7. a
8. b

B
1. the young lady
2. insarcophagusment
3. site
4. two plots
5. Caucasians
6. the sack of body suspended and the face above it with eyes red and horribly starting from their sockets
7. the upper part of the body

C
2. h
3. k
4. e
5. a
6. m
7. i
8. b
9. g
10. c
11. j
12. l
13. f

The Praying Businessman *page 92*

A
1. Make us successful.
2. in getting this hotel
3. called the St. Gregory
4. We ask
5. In addition, if this is what you want
6. We want it done quickly and at a good price.
7. We ask for your blessing
8. Have them be reasonable.

B
1. a
2. b
3. b
4. a
5. b

A Shorter Workweek? No! *page 97*

A
1. b
2. a
3. b
4. b
5. b

B
1. The shorter workweek destroys the eight-hour day which unions have fought for. Management will make a higher profit by cutting overtime costs.
2. Organizations will use it as a cure for absenteeism and turnover rather than make jobs more interesting and challenging.
3. Fixed employee costs would increase. Increased prices would reduce the demand for goods and a recession cycle would begin.

4. Workers would seek additional part-time work and would keep some of the unemployed from getting jobs.
5. There are only 35 hours of production in the workweek now because of coffee breaks, long weekends, etc.
6. There is enough leisure time already. Too much leisure is not good.

Selling America *page 100*

A
1. a
2. b
3. a
4. b
5. a
6. b

B
1. b
2. a
3. b
4. a
5. a

C
Landesfahr: The consumer doesn't think. He's just one big gaping jaw to cram things into.
Landesfahr: All products are identical, but ad men make up reasons why their product is better.
Landesfahr: You can condition people to buy what you want them to buy.

"Big John": Chicago's complete city in the sky *page 105*

B
1. F
2. DS
3. F
4. DS
5. T
6. DS
7. F
8. DS
9. F
10. T
11. DS
12. F
13. DS
14. F

VI. SOCIAL SCENES

A Teenager Looks for Work *page 110*

A
1. a
2. b
3. b
4. a

Kids' Country *page 112*

B
1. b
2. c
3. b
4. c
5. a
6. c

Making a Future *page 114*

A
1. Shipping clerk, salesman, businessman.
2. He works on a farm.
3. He likes being outdoors and working with horses.
4. He thinks that he isn't doing anything with his life—he is wasting his time.

C
1. all you really desire is to be outdoors, with your shirt off. (paragraph 4)
2. This farm I work on, it's spring there now. (paragraph 6)
3. That's when I come running home./ It's spring there now. (paragraph 6)

D a

The Terrible People *page 116*

A c; Line 5

B
3

C
1. stealthy
2. a handsome annuity
3. to make both ends meet

4. burden
5. blessing
6. incurable

Hollywood, Hollywood *page 118*

A
1. a
2. b
3. b
4. a
5. a
6. b
7. a
8. a
9. a
10. b

Blue Jeans Culture *page 123*

A
1. F
2. F
3. T
4. T
5. T
6. T
7. T
8. T

Car Culture *page 125*

A 2

C
1. c
2. c

What Is Art? *page 127*

A
1. b
2. b
3. a
4. b
5. a
6. b

CONTRIBUTORS

We would like to thank Ellen Moskowitz, Director of the Ethnic Studies Project at Queens College, Flushing, New York 11367, and J. Rupert Picott, Executive Director of the Association for the Study of Afro-American Life and History, Inc., 1407 Fourteenth Street, NW, Washington, D.C. 20005, for their assistance in compiling data for the chart on page 41.